The Inside Guide to Being

Also available from Continuum

Behavioural, Emotional and Social Difficulties: A Guide for the Early Years, Janet Kay

Childminder's Handbook, Allison Lee

Childminder's Guide to Play and Activities, Allison Lee

Co-ordinating Special Educational Needs: A Guide for the Early Years, Damien Fitzgerald

Getting Your Little Darlings to Behave, Sue Cowley

Good Practice in the Early Years, Janet Kay

Help Your Child with Literacy, Caroline Coxon

Help Your Child with Numeracy, Rosemary Russell

Medical Conditions: A Guide for the Early Years, Pam Dewis

Observing Children and Young People, Carole Sharman, Wendy Cross and Diana Vennis

Protecting Children, Janet Kay

Contents list

Introduction

Childminding is an exciting career with varied roles and many prospects.

To be a successful childminder you will need to know how to care for children, keep them safe, nurture them, entertain them, educate them, befriend them, placate them, nurse them and feed them. You will also need to know how to run your own business successfully. Childminding can be a demanding and often exhausting profession, but the rewards are very high – it can offer true job satisfaction!

Childminders need great 'people skills'. You will need to be able to relate to the children's families and have the personality to be able to get on with people from a wide range of backgrounds. You will also need to be confident in all areas concerned with running a small business, such as planning and organizing, managing your accounts and bookkeeping, together with keeping abreast of all essential training relevant to the profession.

This book has been written to offer you an insight into all aspects of being a childminder and to offer guidance and support, from one professional to another. Each of the chapters will help you plan for all scenarios to make for the smooth running of your business.

Childminding can at times be nerve-racking and relentless but it is also enjoyable, exciting and great fun! Juggling family commitments and work commitments by taking up a career in childminding can be a wonderful solution for many people.

1

The role of the childminder

Gone are the days when childminders were seen as uneducated, low-paid babysitters who were paid to 'keep an eye on the children' whilst their parents went to work. The world has changed and with it the need for good quality childcare has arisen. Parents are no longer content to pay someone to look after their child because they appear motherly and seem to like playing with children. Parents now, quite rightly, express a wish to find a highly qualified, organized person who has the right skills not only to nurture their child but to educate and discipline them. A childminder's role is varied and can be described in a number of ways.

The Carer

Whilst working as a childminder your role will involve being a carer for children. Parents will expect you to care for their children as you would your own. You will have the responsibility of making sure that the children are safe at all times when they are with you and you will be expected to be aware of and remove any potential hazards. You will need to know how to comfort a child when they are upset, appease them when they are angry and entertain them when they are bored.

The Teacher

It is generally believed that the sooner a child starts with their education the brighter they will be. This is reflected by the training offered to childminders to enhance their skills, and also by the Early Years Foundation Stage (www.everychildmatters.gov.uk).

The hours you work as a childminder and the ages of the children you care for will have a great influence on how you carry out your role as an educator. If you care for pre-school children you will need to be equipped with the knowledge necessary to enable you to promote the statutory framework for the Early Years Foundation Stage (for more information go to the Early Years Foundation Stage guidance in the Teaching and Learning section of www.teachernet.gov.uk). If you also provide care for school-aged children it will be useful for you to be aware of the topics being taught in school and you should familiarize yourself with the methods currently being taught with regard to how children learn to read and write and how numeracy skills are promoted – these have changed a great deal since most of us were at school! (See the Primary and Secondary sections of Teaching and Learning on the website www.teachernet.gov.uk for further guidance.)

The Behaviourist

Getting children to behave some of the time is difficult; getting them to behave all of the time is nigh on impossible! So the most important thing you must remember first and foremost is that children will misbehave. No child is perfect (regardless of what their parents would like you to believe!) and all children will, at some point, push the boundaries and see how far they are allowed to go.

Supervising young children is not always easy and you will need to be confident in behaviour management. Not all children are adept at mixing with others and sometimes the children in your care may have little in common and may clash at every opportunity. You will be expected to manage this type of behaviour and encourage the children to form friendships and learn to get along.

You may get a child to look after who thinks that they can do anything they like 'because my mummy pays you'. (Believe it or not I have had five-year olds who have come to my home genuinely believing that they can treat me disrespectfully because their parents pay my wages!) As a childminder, it is important to instill values and respect in the children in your care as part of your role. Admittedly this is not always easy when caring for someone else's children as what may be acceptable in one person's home may be totally unacceptable in another's. It is important therefore that you ensure that all the parents and children you care for are aware of your own values from the very start. To command respect you will have to earn it. Start as you mean to go on and set out rules which everyone will need to be aware of. (For further guidance, refer to Chapter 10, Writing and implementing policies.)

Many toddlers will go through the tantrum stage – 'the terrible twos' – however it is how this stage of their behaviour is managed and dealt with that will determine whether the child grows out of the tantrums and learns what is socially acceptable or continues to demand attention through loud, violent outbursts.

I am not an advocate of the 'naughty corner' – apologies Supernanny! – I have yet to find a child who feels any remorse after busting his brother's nose knowing full well the only punishment he is likely to receive is a couple of minutes in the naughty corner, no doubt sniggering behind his hand as his sibling is comforted by the childminder. The best way to respond to unwanted behaviour is through consistency. I have a simple set of rules that are easy for all the children in my care to understand, and importantly which their parents are aware of, and I am consistent with the way I deal with unwanted behaviour. When I say 'no' I mean 'no' and I am not open to persuasion; I cannot be coerced or cajoled, as I know that this will result in the child continually pushing the boundaries and over-stepping the mark in the belief that they will eventually get their own way.

In worst case scenarios where I might find myself caring for a child whose behaviour I simply cannot manage, no matter what I try, I would give that child's parents notice to take the child out of my setting. This would of course be a last resort and I would endeavour to try all avenues, working in partnership with the child's parents, before doing something so drastic. Yet, in the interests of everyone involved, it is better to cut your losses and admit that you are not right for each other thus allowing the parents to find childcare more suited to their child's needs.

The Chef

As a childminder, your role (depending on the service you choose to offer – see Chapter 7 for more information) might also involve providing meals for the children in your care – breakfast, lunch and/or dinner depending on the times you are working. As we all know children will not always eat anything you throw at them! They may eat you out of house and home if you continually offer the kind of unhealthy foods they invariably love such as crisps, chocolate and biscuits, but this kind of menu will not please the child's parents or meet the national standards you are required to work to, even if it does keep the children happy! You will need to understand all about healthy eating. This is not just as simple as knowing how many portions of fruit and vegetables a child should be eating every day – it will also involve knowing how to *disguise* these very portions in order to encourage the children to actually eat them!

You will also need to bear in mind the requests of parents for their children's meals and work to ensure that you are able to provide food that is suitable for all, including yourself as chef! 'Melissa loves her meat' and 'Danny needs at least four pieces of fruit a day to maintain a healthy diet' will be just a couple of the things that parents might say to you when giving their *preferred* menu to you, detailing gourmet meals consisting of organic food stuffs, but you will need to weigh up the costs involved and make sure your books still balance if you wish to provide the same! On the other hand burgers and chips may be the child's staple diet in some homes but whilst they are in your care this will not be appropriate.

To get around the problems which may arise at meal times I make sure that I know exactly which foods each child likes and dislikes and I try to offer a varied diet taking these preferences into account. I ask parents for a list of foods their child prefers, tolerates and absolutely loathes and bear this in mind when preparing meals!

It is a good idea to stick with a tried and tested menu and vary this from week to week. If you wish to have a set menu, make sure that you rotate your meals and, instead of preparing a weekly set menu, it may be better to have a fortnightly or monthly cycle to avoid the same foods being served on the same day every week as this may become boring, particularly if some children are only in your setting for one day of the week and are being served the same meal all the time.

Always stick to fresh produce as much as possible and if, like me, you choose to make your own baby foods from scratch rather than buy prepared jars, then never add salt or sugar to the recipes.

When providing mid-morning or afternoon snacks for the children make sure you offer a variety of fresh fruit, juice and water rather than biscuits and fizzy drinks.

Visit www.organix.com for ideas for baby and toddler foods together with menu ideas which can be downloaded.

The Nurse

'Jemima has been awake all night crying, I don't know what's wrong with her but I'm sure you'll know what to do!' This kind of scenario seems absurd but it is quite common for the average childminder. It may be that it simply hasn't occurred to the parent that their child may be in need of medical assistance but more often it is a case of the parent not having time to think things through and take time off work to make a doctor's appointment, so they bring their child to the childminder expecting them to perform miracles! Many parents will tell you that their child isn't unwell but that there is a 'bottle of paracetamol' in the child's bag 'just in case'!

First aid training, which is compulsory for all childminders, will put you in good stead when carrying out your role of 'nurse', but you must know your limits and, if you are in any doubt whatsoever, you must seek medical advice.

(For further guidance on putting together a policy on whether you will look after children who are ill, refer to Chapter 10. Guidance on first aid training is given in Chapter 2.)

The Cleaner

Sadly, providing a childcare service is not all about playing with and entertaining children. Unlike teachers and nursery staff who, when the children have gone home, can leave the unenviable task of cleaning the classroom to the cleaning staff, you will have to perform yet another duty. After having worked a ten-hour day teaching, supervising and nursing the children, you fall into the chair after the last child has gone home and look around your house through exhausted eyes. The baking session, which seemed such a good idea only a couple of hours ago and which the children enjoyed immensely, has left your kitchen looking as if a bomb has hit it. You reel at the play dough ground into your carpet and the paint spattered on your walls and wonder if it was all worth the effort. Well of course it was! The children have had a wonderful day and have gone home with exciting stories to tell their parents and freshly iced cup cakes for supper so what's a bit of flour on the floor or paint on the walls – everything cleans right? Out comes the vacuum cleaner and the cleaning materials and an hour later your home is looking as good as new ready for the next day's relentless onslaught. Junk modelling and papier mâché wasn't it?!

The Supervisor

Supervising children effectively is something which will come with practice and experience. To supervise you will need to know the children well and be aware of when to sit back and watch and when to become actively involved. Children need to feel that they have achieved something for themselves – this is how their confidence and self-esteem is built up and you will need to know which activities to provide and when to offer support and assistance. (For further guidance refer to the *Childminder's Guide to Play and Activities* by Allison Lee, Continuum 2007.)

The Friend

This is a difficult one but by no means impossible. Despite the fact that you are running a business and as such will need to keep some things on a business footing, it is also possible to become good friends with the children you care for and their families. Indeed in many cases being a friend is what childminding is all about. Childminding offers a much more personal service than a large day nursery and in welcoming the parents and children into your home each day you will need to have respect for one another and this will, hopefully, grow into a valued friendship. Many childminders remain in touch with the families long after the children have grown up and left the setting.

However it is important that you ensure that by becoming a 'family friend' you are not putting yourself in the position of becoming the 'family mug'! Don't allow your friendship to stop you pointing out if you haven't been paid on time or if the parents are collecting their child later and later each day resulting in you working several hours unpaid overtime each week. These issues need addressing and, if your friendship is to be effective and valued, it has to work both ways. All give from the childminder will leave them feeling resentful and used. Never allow yourself to become a martyr and always address issues as and when they arise.

So there you have it! Some of the varied roles of the average childminder. The list above is by no means exhaustive and there are many other roles you will need to be proficient in if your business is to be successful such as:

1   Entertainer

2   Noise controller

3   Speech therapist

4   Builder

5   Hygienist

6   Receptionist

7   Dishwasher

8   Nappy changer

9 Storyteller

10 Nose wiper

11 Problem solver

12 Accountant

13 Musician.

When you decide to become a childminder it is absolutely vital that you understand that the job most definitely does *not* entail simply 'minding' children. If you like a job which offers you the opportunity to meet new people and experience an enormous amount of variety then childminding is what you are looking for!

Useful websites

www.ofsted.gov.uk
Office for Standards in Education (Ofsted)

www.surestart.gov.uk
SureStart, the government programme that brings together early education, childcare, health and family support. Search the Publications section of this site for the government's national standards relating to childminding.

www.teachernet.gov.uk
A teacher's website that offers full guidance on all aspects of education. The Teaching and Learning section is particularly useful, for guidance on the Early Years Foundation Stage (0–5 years) and for guidance on what is going on at schools to help in your planning of activities.

2

Essential training for the job

If you think that the only training you will need for the job of a childminder is to know how to stop a baby from crying and change a nappy then think again!

Although even changing a nappy as a childminder is not as straightforward and simple as you might imagine – you will need to don apron and gloves before attempting to handle any smelly bundles – this is by far the least of your training requirements.

The Diploma in Home-based Childcare

There is a certain amount of compulsory training which childminders need to undertake and, in addition, you may like to enrol on a variety of other courses designed to assist you in your work. Childminders are obliged to enrol on an introductory training course within six months of their registration. The National Childminding Association (NCMA) and the Council for Awards in Children's Care and Education (CACHE) launched the Diploma in Home-based Childcare (DHC) in January 2006. (This diploma is an updated version of the previous qualification, the Certificate in Childminding Practice (CCP), and the main difference is that the new diploma is suitable for all *home-based child carers* including nannies.) The Diploma in Home-based Childcare consists of five separate units, but only Unit 1, the Introduction to Childcare Practice in the Home-based Setting, is actually compulsory.

Childminders will either have already completed Unit 1 or will be enrolled on the course when they begin childminding. However, if they then choose to continue with their training and decide to complete the CCP they will usually be doing this whilst carrying out their childminding duties. Evening classes and distance-learning programmes are available for practitioners who cannot attend daytime lessons due to their childminding commitments.

The first unit of the DHC consists of 12 guided learning hours, whilst the remaining four units consist of 30 guided learning hours each. Certificates are issued after each unit is completed but in order to gain the complete Diploma all five units must be successfully undertaken.

The five units which make up the Diploma in Home-based Childcare are as follows:

- Unit 1: Introduction to Childcare Practice in the Home-based Setting

- Unit 2: Childcare and Child Development (0–16) in the Home-based Setting

- Unit 3: The Childcare Practitioner in the Home-based Setting

- Unit 4: Working in Partnership with Parents in the Home-based Setting

- Unit 5: Planning to Meet Children's Individual Learning Needs in the Home-based Setting.

Unit 1: Introduction to Childcare Practice (ICP) Home-based

This unit is compulsory for all new childminders who are just starting out in their chosen profession. Unit 1 is designed to help childcare practitioners to:

1   Assess the home-based setting for risks and ensure a safe and healthy environment is provided.

2   Introduce planning routines, settle children into their care and manage behaviour effectively.

3   Provide play and other activities suitable for children in a home-based setting.

4   Prepare and promote good relationships with parents and other primary carers.

5   Establish routines for home-based childcare.

6   Look at their responsibilities with regard to children who may be suffering from abuse or neglect.

7   Prepare for the setting up of their childcare service and ensure that any legal requirements are met.

Unit 1 is assessed by 25 multiple-choice questions which you will need to submit for external marking by CACHE. The marking system for Unit 1 means that you will either gain a 'pass' or a 'referral'. In order to ensure that this method of assessment is fair to all candidates, a different set of questions are prepared and issued by CACHE on a monthly basis. The 25 questions are designed to test your knowledge on the areas listed above and to ensure that you are confident about what you have learned. In order to pass Unit 1 you will need to give correct answers for a set number of questions, and failure to do this will result in a 'referral'. If you are referred this means that you have not answered enough questions correctly to achieve a pass and you will need to re-enter for assessment. You will be given a different set of questions for your second referral, and for any subsequent referrals you may need.

Unit 2: Childcare and Child Development (0–16) in the Home-based Setting

This unit will help practitioners to think about:

1   Children's development and well-being

2   Working with disabled children and their families

3   Promoting children's rights.

Unit 3: The Childcare Practitioner in the Home-based Setting

This unit will help practitioners to think about:

1   Being reflective

2   Being assertive and knowing how to value their own self-worth

3   Advertising and marketing their childcare service

4   Working with other professionals

5   Writing and implementing policies

6   Child protection issues

7   Continuing professional development.

Unit 4: Working in Partnership with Parents in the Home-based Setting

This unit will help practitioners to think about:

1   Families in general

2   Different cultures

3   Confidentiality, data protection and the law

4   Communication with parents and primary carers

5   Building positive relationships with parents and primary carers

6   Contracts

7   Complaints.

Unit 5: Planning to Meet Children's Individual Learning Needs in the Home-based Setting

This unit will help practitioners to think about:

1   Meeting individual learning needs

2   Preparing, implementing and evaluating plans for home-based groups of children of different ages and abilities

3   Observing and assessing children's development.

There is some form of assessment for each of the five units that make up the DHC and, in order to achieve the full award, you will need to complete successfully each unit at a minimum of grade E. However Unit 1 is an exception to this grading system and is marked as either 'pass' or 'refer' (see previous information regarding Unit 1).

Units 2–5 each have a separate assessment that is set by CACHE and these assignments will be marked by a tutor. These four units are assessed by grade boundaries 'E' to 'A' which are explained below.

The overall grade for Units 2–5 is established by adding up the number of 'points' achieved for each assessment based on the following ranges:

Grade A   19–21 points

Grade B   15–18 points

Grade C	11–14 points
Grade D	8–10 points
Grade E	5–7 points

Generally speaking, you will be awarded higher marks if you can demonstrate to your tutor that you have fully understood the questions posed and by providing as much correct information as possible. You will need to think carefully about your written assessments in order to include the correct *relevant* information as there will be a word limit involved.

UNIT	GRADE E	GRADE D	GRADE C	GRADE B	GRADE A
2	1 point	2 points	3 points	4 points	5 points
3	1 point	2 points	3 points	4 points	5 points
4	1 point	2 points	3 points	4 points	5 points
5	1 point	2 points	3 points	4 points	5 points

The overall grade on the final certificate will be taken from the grades you are awarded for each of the four units. For example, using the table above, if you achieved:

Grade C for Unit 2 you would have gained 3 points

Grade B for Unit 3 you would have gained 4 points

Grade A for Unit 4 you would have gained 5 points

Grade B for Unit 5 you would have gained 4 points

By adding together the number of 'points' you have gained for each unit (3 + 4 + 5 + 4 = 16 points) you can see that you would have achieved 16 points which, using the information above, would give you an overall grade of 'B' on your final certificate.

It is possible to upgrade your work if you wish to achieve a higher mark by resubmitting it. However this can only be done once. If you initially received a 'C' grade and would like to see if you can improve on this you will be allowed to resubmit your work. You will not be awarded a mark *lower* than your initial grade although it is possible that, even after re-submitting your assignment, you may still end up with the same grade.

KEY POINTS TO CONSIDER:

- Do not rush – make sure that you are well prepared and that you have understood everything before attempting any of the assessments. There is nothing like a 'pass' or 'A' grade to boost your confidence. However consider how your confidence will take a knock if you end up with a 'referral'.

- Don't struggle if you do not understand something. Talk to your tutor if you are unsure of anything – that is what they are there for!

- Read and re-read all the questions and (in the case of Unit 1) possible answers carefully *before* attempting to complete the assessments. Often silly mistakes are made by not reading questions correctly and this can result in the loss of vital points.

The DHC can be completed either in a classroom or through enrolling with a distance learning college. There are pros and cons to each method of learning. Having studied for qualifications both in a classroom and through distance learning, the latter proved more successful for me. Most childminders, unless they have opted to work part-time, will work very long hours. It is not unusual for our day to begin at 7.30am and finish well after 6pm and going on to a two-hour lesson at college might not be appealing to many!

So I would recommend distance learning to anyone who is expected to give their all from Monday to Friday. However, distance learning does require a great deal of discipline. Not everyone will want to study on a weekend or when they get a spare hour or two during the evening, which is what will be required of you.

Should you choose this route, however, you might find that you can get more done working two hours at home than you can spending two hours in a classroom, which involves travel time.

However, on the flipside, a benefit of studying for such courses in colleges and the like is that it will give you an environment to share your ideas and learning with others in the same situation. In childminding, rarely do we have the opportunity to share ideas and views in our daily working lives and we must learn to think for ourselves and follow the courage of our convictions. We need to know how to run a business successfully and to use our own thoughts and initiatives, so you may find comfort in setting out by studying with others, or you might enjoy the challenge of working alone from the beginning, starting as you mean to go on. It is important to choose the route that works best for you. Tutors are always at hand if you are struggling and there is no need for any student to feel their way blindly through a course.

Cost is of course one of the pitfalls of distance learning, and although many authorities will fund the cost of a course attended in college not all will stretch their funds to pay for students to study via distance learning. Contact your local authority for information regarding funding for courses and enquire whether this funding covers both classroom-based and distance learning. Information regarding the cost of courses, including the DHC through distance learning, can be found by contacting The National Extension College on www.nec.ac.uk or by telephoning them on 01223 400 200.

Further details of the Diploma in Home-based Childcare can be obtained by contacting the Council for Awards in Children's Care and Education (CACHE) on www.cache.org.uk or you can telephone them on 0845 347 2123.

Quality Assurance

Many authorities now offer childminders the chance to enrol on a Quality Assurance scheme. Quality Assurance schemes require the childminder to develop a portfolio of evidence which shows that they meet high-quality standards in their practice. The National Childminding Association (NCMA) launched Quality First in 2003. Quality First is a nationally recognized quality assurance scheme for individual registered childminders and ensures, among other things, that childminders have:

1   Proved that they are committed to working towards the NCMA's ten Quality Standards.

2   Produced a portfolio showing that they provide a good quality service and they reflect on their practice in order to find ways of continuing to improve on the service they offer.

3   Had their service checked by an NCMA assessor who has satisfied him or herself that the childminder communicates with and relates to the children satisfactorily.

Quality First can be undertaken at any one of three levels, Level 1 being the easiest to achieve.

Being assessed is by far the most important way for childminders to prove that the service they provide meets with the standards set out. After all anyone can build up a portfolio and *say* that they will provide the children in their care with a good standard of care but how does anyone actually know that this is the case? Assessors are very astute and they can usually tell very early on how well a childminder knows the children in their care and how happy and content the children are. The assessor will look at how approachable the childminder is, how they deal with everyday incidents, how they interact with the children and how they ensure that all the children's needs are met.

Further there is one thing we can almost certainly be sure of, and that is the honesty of a child. Children will speak their minds whether this is appropriate or not and, be warned, anyone trying to pull the wool over an assessor's eyes will be in for a rough ride. If the snack you usually offer the children consists of chocolate biscuits and fizzy pop don't be surprised if they complain when the assessor is present because you have substituted this for fresh fruit and water; rest assured they *will* moan and ask for the 'usual snack that we always have'. Don't try to go out of your way to impress the assessor. If you are doing your job well anyway this won't be necessary and if you aren't doing your job well it is highly unlikely that you will have enrolled to do a Quality Assurance Scheme in the first place!

Quality Assurance offers childminders a number of benefits such as:

1   Offering the practitioner opportunities for development.

2   Promoting quality day care and education.

3   Enabling the practitioner to demonstrate their commitment to their profession and is particularly useful when preparing for the Ofsted inspection.

4   Enabling the practitioner to evaluate their own setting and working practice.

5   Setting clear aims and objectives.

Choosing to become a part of a Quality Assurance scheme gives the childminder the opportunity to access a wealth of resources, enables them to take part in support meetings and links them with a mentor and Quality Assurance manager.

Child protection

It is a sad fact of life that not all children are blessed with the happy secure home life that they deserve and, unfortunately, it is necessary for childminders to have a sound understanding of child protection issues. Despite efforts by the government, the number of children being placed on child protection registers each year is on the increase. Neglect is the most common reason for a child to be placed on the register, followed by physical abuse.

Childminders are not obliged to enrol on any compulsory courses relating to child protection issues. Although Unit 1 of the DHC briefly looks at child protection in the home-based setting and focuses on the signs and symptoms of abuse, it is not until practitioners enrol on Unit 3 that child protection is covered in more detail, but it is not a compulsory unit.

All childminders should be competent in recognizing and dealing with child protection issues regardless of whether they are likely to come across these types of issues regularly or not. If there is the slightest *chance* of a child being in danger then those responsible for their care and education should be aware of the procedures to follow. Childminders, unlike schools and nurseries, do not have anyone else to turn to if they suspect a child is being mistreated and they must rely on their own training and ability to guide them.

Although childminders must be competent when recognizing the signs and symptoms of abuse and know which procedures to follow should they suspect any mistreatment of a child in their care they must also be very careful not to misread the signs.

Bumps, bruises and cuts are injuries that all children will receive at some point in their lives and receiving the odd scrape is all part of growing up. I would, in fact, be more worried if a child *never* showed any signs of having suffered a fall or bump as this would point to the fact that they were not allowed to explore or take risks which is, of course, essential to a child's development.

Knowing which injuries are a result of an innocent fall, and which are signs of something more sinister, is something that all childcare practitioners should be competent in recognizing. There is no denying that this is a difficult task and one which many childminders worry about.

Common sites for *accidental* injuries

Usually injuries to the following areas of the body can be classed as accidental although of course not all injuries to these body parts may be innocent.

1   Forehead

2   Chin

3   Nose

4   Shins

5   Knees

6   Spine

7   Hips

8   Elbows

9   Forearms.

Common sites for *non-accidental* injuries

Injuries to the following areas of the body *may* need to be looked at in ways other than accidental.

1   Lips

2   Mouth

3   Cheeks

4   Ears

5   Skull

6   Stomach

7   Chest

8   Back

9   Buttocks

10   Genital or rectal areas

11   Back of the legs

12   Upper or inner arms

13   Soles of the feet.

You will need to be very careful when assessing a child's injuries and deciding whether they are a result of an innocent accident or a result of the child being abused. Factors such as the regularity and the severity of the injury should be taken into account. Explanations, if any, offered by the child or their parent should also be taken into consideration. Never be afraid to ask a parent how a child has received an injury and always record serious injuries along with the parents' explanation to cover yourself – occasionally childminders have been falsely accused of harming children in order to cover up cases of abuse. Getting parents to sign your written record of the injury will prevent any such allegations.

First aid

In Chapter 1 of this book we looked at the roles of the childminder. One of those roles was 'nurse'. I purposely stopped short of adding doctor, life saver and surgeon for fear of putting the squeamish off. However if the sight of blood leaves you cold and the sound of snapping bones gives you shivers down your spine then perhaps you ought to stock up on the cotton wool now and, the minute the children walk through your door, wrap them securely in a huge blanket!

Children will invariably succumb to accidents when on your premises. It is down to you to eliminate any potential dangers as far as is possible, but stopping short of placing the child in a padded cell void of any toys or equipment you cannot eliminate *every* danger. Bumps and bruises are all part of growing up and children should be allowed to explore their environment as much as possible, preferably stopping short of allowing them to climb up the chimney breast to 'see where the smoke goes'!

Unlike many other areas of training, first aid is a *compulsory* requirement for any childminder. You will be expected to enrol on a course specializing in paediatric first aid and this course must be for a minimum of 12 hours in order to successfully cover all aspects of accidents and emergencies. First aid certificates usually last for three years and you will be required to enrol on a refresher course before your existing certificate expires.

It is good practice to refresh what you have learned periodically and it can also be a good idea to practise certain areas of first aid, such as the recovery position, with the children in your care so that they too can be aware of what to do in an emergency.

Remember, it is essential that you know your limitations and that medical attention is sought immediately if you are in any doubt about the seriousness of the child's injury.

We have all walked out of our first aid class with blue lips having tried to give a rubber doll the kiss of life. The doll may resemble a child in size and weight but believe me this is where the similarities end and when faced with a lifeless child the very last thing you will be worrying about is how much pressure you put on your own lips in order to breathe life into the body. Recap on mouth to mouth resuscitation and compressions as much as you feel is necessary so that you will know exactly what to do should an emergency arise.

I am not going to say 'don't panic' when you are faced with an emergency because this is a waste of time. Of course you will panic. It is human nature, when faced with this kind of situation. However it is absolutely vital that you stay as calm as possible and deal with the situation methodically in order to minimize the risk to the other people present and assist the injured person. Prior careful planning and a sound knowledge in first aid should help you to deal with any accidents and emergencies efficiently and if you are worried about your ability to deal with this type of situation it is important that you enrol on a refresher course.

The way in which you handle an emergency situation will have a profound effect on the outcome. You can either:

1   Quickly assess the situation and minimize the risk of danger to yourself and others.

2   Offer reassurance.

3   Stay in control.

4 Carry out the emergency procedures you have been taught and which you have rehearsed and know well.

Or you can:

1 Scream

2 Panic

3 Faint.

Hopefully you will choose the first option!

Optional training

In addition to the above training there are numerous other courses and workshops which childminders can access in order to gain vital knowledge and experience. Your local authority will be able to furnish you with details of training and workshops which cover topics such as:

- Business training – important for managing finances, marketing your business and bookkeeping

- Food hygiene

- Introducing babies to books

- Understanding and using empathy dolls

- Learning about the importance of the outdoor environment

- Working with children with special needs

- Understanding, producing and utilizing treasure baskets.

The National Childminding Association also holds various area, regional and national conferences throughout the year offering childminders the chance to meet other practitioners and take part in workshops designed to assist them in their work such as:

- Safety and fire prevention
- Healthy eating
- Festival foods
- Diversity within the setting
- Exploring the senses
- Getting ready for your Ofsted inspection
- Policies and procedures.

Details of all forthcoming conferences and events can be found by visiting the National Childminding Association's website www.ncma.org.uk or looking at their quarterly magazine 'Who Minds?' Local authorities also organize useful workshops and seminars, most of which are funded, for childminders and these can be a very successful way of accessing vital information. Contact your own local authority for further details.

3
Skills needed for the job

In addition to the paper certificates you will receive proving that you are competent in first aid, have gained a Diploma in Home-based Childcare and successfully completed a Quality Assurance Scheme there are several more very important skills that you will require in order to become a successful childminder.

Patience

Patience is a virtue. However, when you are the only person appearing to show any, it can sometimes be a curse! Children can and will test the patience of a saint. If they think their behaviour isn't bothering you this will rarely discourage them – the simple truth is they will try even harder to gain your attention.

Young children are often messy, noisy and boisterous with mucus-dripping nostrils and smelly nappies and, unless you are Mother Teresa, they will invariably test your patience at some point. Childminding is a stressful job and, the more children you care for, the more stressful it becomes so it is important for you to learn how to relax. You will need to know when to rise to a challenge and when to let things go.

Before deciding how many children you would like to provide care for and, more importantly, what ages you would like to cater for, it is important to think things through carefully. It is all too easy to see each child as potential profit, after all it goes without saying that the more children you care for the more money you will make, but making money, though important when running a business, is not the only aspect you should be considering. By taking on lots of children you may actually be doing yourself more harm than good. The more children you cater for the more demanding your job will be. However, in childminding, it does not always follow that the more customers you have the more profit you will make. You may be caring for seven children under the age of eight years, for example. However, if five of these children attend school and the other two are only part-time placements you will probably earn less money than if you cared for just three children under school age full-time. The more children you care for the higher your outgoings will be as you will need to feed these children, entertain them and provide them with activities and resources. Seven children will invariably eat and drink more than three!

If you have patience by the bucketful then by all means consider taking on the maximum number of children your registration permits you to. However, if you are unsure of exactly what is involved and just how much mess and mayhem young children create then you would be well advised to take things slowly, pace yourself and start with one or two children before slowly building your business up to suit your own preferences, lifestyle and stress limits!

Patience is not just needed when dealing with children. At times it will also be necessary for you to be patient with parents. It is important to remember that all families are different and parenting styles vary tremendously. You will not always agree with the way a parent cares for their child and you will need to show patience, among other virtues in these cases. New parents in particular, who are finding their feet and are unsure of how to care for their offspring, may appear to have little idea about feeding patterns, sleep etc. Show as much patience as you possibly can in these cases. Never criticize but offer lots of support, only giving advice if you are asked for it to avoid risking interfering.

Stamina

As a childminder you will be expected to be available all day every day. Don't fool yourself into thinking you will be allowed to take a couple of days off if you are sick – childminders simply do not have time to be ill! – and if they do their bank balance will suffer considerably and woe betide any childminder who insists on being paid if they are ill, even if the illness is a direct result of having cared for a sick child! You will get some parents who will sympathize with your predicament whilst muttering under their breath how utterly inconvenient your illness is. There will be some who insist that your own husband take time off from his job to care for their children whilst you are unable to. There will be others – very few – who will insist on paying you, tell you to take yourself off to bed and take as much time off as you need. The latter is all well and done but if you care for children from several families sadly you will *rarely* experience this kind of reaction from all of them!

The simple truth of the matter is that most childminders succumb to an average of two days' sick leave for every ten years' service and even then they will not be allowed to forget how much trouble they have caused. Becoming ill is, you would imagine, one of the easiest ways to prove to parents how invaluable your service is to them. By not being available you cause them a problem and make them sit up and think about just how much they rely on you. This *should* make them value your service even more, but instead it is more likely that it will make them consider using a nursery so they won't have to worry about sickness cover in the future!

Of course stamina is not just about refusing to succumb to illness. The physical efforts of being a childminder pale in comparison to the mental efforts. Childminding is *physically* taxing – you will be on the go all day every day chasing around after children, clearing up, playing, collecting children from various schools, playgroups and clubs, but the *mental* side of childminding is far, far more draining. You will need to please everyone as much as possible. You may be caring for five or six children from different families. Not only must you keep these children happy but each will probably have a mother and father who will also expect you to keep them happy – and at times will be much more demanding than any child – so all in all you may end up trying to please 18 people every day. Add on grandparents, aunties and uncles who invariably like to give their opinion on the service you provide and you will be ready to make an appointment to see a psychiatrist sooner rather than later! Being prepared for this, and being able to be resilient and take everything in your stride will set you in good stead.

Planning and organization

This is the area where a lot of childminders, both experienced and newly qualified, come unstuck. When they make the decision to work from home, looking after children, they do not anticipate the work involved in the planning and organization of their daily routine.

Effective planning and good organizational skills are the key to running a successful childminding business. If you are the kind of person who decides what to have for lunch three minutes before beginning to prepare it then you are going to have to change. Caring for young children is a time-consuming occupation and, in order for everything to run smoothly, you will need to be organized.

Ideally you will plan for each day the night before. At first this may mean planning meals and activities at midnight but if you don't want to be faced with six hungry children all waiting for their breakfast and find that you have run out of milk and bread then this will be necessary. Given time and a little experience you will soon learn how to plan effectively. You may make a few mistakes along the way – after all didn't someone once say we all learn by our mistakes? There is a lot of planning involved in a childminder's daily routine. You will need to plan around:

Your daily routine

Your daily routine will be hectic and many childminders spend a vast amount of their day out and about (well at least this keeps the house tidy!) taking children to school, playgroup and nursery and then collecting again. You may make weekly trips to the library, toddler group, support group or play gym and of course the times and days for these will have to be incorporated into your routine. For example, you would be unable to plan a trip to the park at 3pm if one of the children is being collected from your house half an hour later.

Feeding times for babies

Babies are *very* trying and you will need to plan for their feeding routines. Look at the essential times you have to keep such as school drop offs and collections and plan the baby's feeds to coincide with these events. There is no excuse for you being late to collect a child from school and explaining that the baby needed her bottle will not go down well with the teachers if you collect children half an hour late.

Mealtimes

These will depend on what time the children arrive at and leave your setting. Try to have specific meal times and stick to them as much as possible. For example. if you give children their breakfast make sure that parents are aware of the time you serve this otherwise you may well find yourself catering for six separate breakfast times. Parents will have been known to drop their child off five minutes before you are due to leave for the school run and ask you to give them breakfast because they 'were up late and didn't have time, you know how Harvey likes his bacon sandwiches'. You also know how impossible it is for Harvey to have his bacon sandwiches five minutes before he is due to set off for school! You would think that parents would bear this in mind but they don't and if they do they consider the problem to be yours to solve anyway. Little Harvey will probably end up with a jam sandwich hastily washed down with a glass of milk and believe me he won't be impressed and neither will his mother when he tells her that evening.

Potty training and nappy changes

This is a difficult one. How can you plan for a child to go to the toilet when they don't even know themselves when they want to go? It is good practice to have set times to check nappies periodically; however it is essential that dirty nappies are changed immediately. There is little point shaking your head disapprovingly at a six-month-old baby who has soiled his nappy 35 minutes before nappy-changing time. Unless you want him to end up with a bottom like a baboon then you would be advised to change him immediately.

Potty training children is a little more difficult. Failure to spot when a child needs the potty results quite simply in a soiled carpet. When your lounge resembles a minefield of wet patches and no one has space to play you might like to think again about your potty-training routine. Sit the child on the potty *regularly* even if they insist they do not need it. Get them used to the potty (but don't be surprised if after having sat on it for 15 minutes and brandishing a bright red halo around the bottom cheeks they wander over to the television and promptly wee all over your DVD collection!).

Paperwork

The paperwork involved in this job is immense. More and more time is being spent on filling in registers and forms and less and less time is left for caring for children. Ideally all your paperwork should be done after the children have gone home. However, in addition to planning, preparation and coursework adding a mountain of paperwork to your evening duties, it theoretically adds another couple of hours to an already long day.

You will be expected to complete on a daily basis:

- An attendance register detailing the times when children arrived at and departed from your setting.

- A diary for each child detailing their feeding/sleeping patterns.

- A journal detailing the activities you provide for the children.

- Daily curriculum plans.

- Medical forms, when necessary, detailing medicine administered and why.

You will be expected to complete on a weekly basis:

- An accounts register giving details of all monies received and spent.

- Weekly curriculum plans.

You will be expected to complete regularly:

- Observations and assessments of the children in your care, the outcome of which must be shared with parents.

- Journals detailing the activities and outings the children enjoy whilst in your care.

- Long-term curriculum plans detailing which areas of the child's development you are focusing on.

Although all of this paperwork can, at first glance, appear daunting, experience will make things easier. The more observations and assessments you carry out, for example, the easier they will be, until you find that they become second nature. After completing registers and journals over a few weeks you will become more and more adept at knowing what information to include and what is unnecessary.

Many childminders dread doing accounts. The best advice I can give anyone when completing accounts is to do them *regularly*. Ideally you should make time to do your accounts every week. Avoid letting things pile up and never allow yourself to go more than a month without updating your accounts book. Keep all receipts and number them. It is far better to log one or two receipts every week and account for half a dozen payments than to wait several months and be faced with dozens of receipts and payments many of which you won't be able to account for. Of course you will need to pay cheques into your bank account and redeem vouchers regularly too if you wish to see any financial rewards for the work you carry out.

Flexibility

One of the main reasons why parents choose childminders as their ideal childcare option is because of their flexibility. The rigid 8am to 6pm opening times of nurseries are often difficult for some parents to meet particularly if they work shifts or unsociable hours. So childminders need to be flexible.

This does not mean, as some parents come to expect, that they are available 24 hours a day, seven days a week. Set your working hours and *stick to them*. If you agreed to work 15-hour days there will always be one parent who turns up late. Give an inch and they will take a hundred miles!

Sadly some parents will wonder why you are making a fuss when they turn up late oblivious to the fact that you have missed your own child's parents' evening at school, or have been unable to attend a concert they have the lead role in. What you must always make clear is that you have set working hours and you are not answerable to parents outside of these. You should not feel that you have to give excuses or reasons for wishing to finish work on time. Parents have been known to do anything and everything before collecting their children from the childminders. I have known mothers who go home and feed the dog and themselves, have a bath and get changed before turning up *late* to collect their children. Genuine reasons for lateness – unavoidable traffic jams, motorway pile-ups, six-foot of snow and unexpected rail strikes – are usually acceptable.

So you need to be flexible. What exactly then does this mean if you are to avoid being taken for a ride? The dictionary's definition of flexible is 'being able to bend easily without breaking'. Broadly speaking then, for a childminder to be flexible it means that they can easily accommodate parental wishes provided their requests do not have any adverse effects on the childminder's own family life. If a parent makes a request that you find difficult to accommodate then it is ok to say so.

You may be expected from time to time to change your arrangements with little notice and provided this can be done without any major complications then you should be willing to do so. If, however, being flexible results in you being unable to meet your other obligations both to the remaining children in your care and your own family then do feel free to say that this isn't possible. Explain your reasons and work together to find a compromise.

Another thing to bear in mind is your availability on the phone outside of working hours. A parent may genuinely think that you do not mind if they telephone you on a Sunday to discuss their child's care for the following week. If you always take their telephone call, spend half an hour in polite conversation with them and tell them that you don't mind being disturbed at the weekend, then you may well have parents telephoning you out of your core working hours on a regular basis; not because they like annoying you but because they genuinely believe that you don't mind, and you have never given them reason to think that you do. If you find yourself with this kind of problem and you *do* mind it is important to be polite but firm. The best way to approach this is to answer their questions initially but let them know that you are not working and that weekends are your personal time; you would prefer to discuss anything relating to childminding during your working hours. Remember that you *do* have the right to time away from your business and being flexible does not mean you are available 24 hours per day.

Tolerance

To a very large extent childminding is all about tolerance. You will often need to show tolerance regarding:

- The way that parents bring up their children. There are many different types of family structure and you will need to accept that parenting comes in a variety of forms.
- The way that parents discipline their children.
- The freedom that parents allow their children.

You may not always agree with the way that parents bring up their children and theoretically this should not pose a problem provided that everyone involved realizes that they may, at times, need to compromise. There is no right or wrong way to bring up a child and what works well for one family structure may be completely wrong for another. However, you should not be expected to show tolerance to the extent that you are actually allowing childminded children to behave in your own home in a way that is unacceptable to you, and in a way that your own children would be chastised for. This is not being tolerant – it is being a doormat!

Assertiveness

Being assertive is something that a lot of people find very difficult. Further, bear in mind that there is a very fine line between being assertive and being aggressive. If you allow parents to set all the rules and take advantage of your good nature you will quickly tire of your job, lose your self-esteem and confidence and feel that you are being taken for granted.

Remember that as a childminder, *you* are responsible for running your own business. *You* set your working days and hours, fees, policies and procedures. And it is *your* responsibility to set up an effective business, rather than that of the parents. The service you decide to offer will either be acceptable or unacceptable to prospective customers. Although at times you may need to be flexible this does not mean that you should allow parents to dictate to you, nor should you alter your setting's policies and procedures to suit one parent if this is clearly unacceptable to yourself and the other families you care for.

Remember it is not possible to please all of the people all of the time and you will be doing yourself a great dis-service if this is something you are aiming to achieve – it is impossible! What you should be aiming for is to provide the best service you possibly can and be confident delivering that service in the best way *you* feel possible.

It is however possible to be assertive, whilst remaining open to other people's views and opinions. Although your childminding business is 'your business' it is important to remember that, without customers, it is worthless. Therefore you need to recognize the importance of compromise and you must respect and value other people's opinions. Always listen to parental wishes and, if you feel you can accommodate them reasonably well without any detrimental effects on yourself or your other customers, then by all means do. Being assertive does not mean having everything your own way and refusing to listen to alternative suggestions; it means being able to recognize the best course of action for you personally and having the courage to carry things through.

Further, when talking to customers, remember to be aware of your own body language at all times. There is little point in trying to tell a parent that something they have requested is not possible if you are timid and unsure, stutter and avoid eye contact. Speak confidently, looking the parent in the eye, and explain why their request cannot be met.

A good listener

Childminders need to be good listeners, which doesn't always come naturally to everyone. It is important when you are listening to what a parent is saying to you that you give them your full attention. Take note of exactly what is being said; monitor and analyse the conversation. Always concentrate when someone is speaking to you, look interested and never interrupt them. This is not always as easy as it first appears! There may be other distractions in the room, your concentration may be diverted or you may also wish to say something which is bothering you. All of these aspects may distract you and distort what is being said. If you are unsure of something that a parent has told you or have not completely understood a request then always say so. It is better to admit you have not understood something than to agree to something which you later find impossible to carry out or, worse still, end up doing wrong.

You could summarize what the parent has said to you at the end of the conversation in order to eliminate any misunderstandings and reiterate exactly what is being meant.

4
Commitment

People go into childminding for a variety of reasons. Some believe that nothing tops the satisfaction of working with young children. Many more have been lured to the idea of running their own business. (Remember though that you will be answerable to many people. Although you are providing a service and therefore you are not actually 'employed' by the parents you are still answerable to them and they will expect a certain amount of professionalism!)

Are you doing the right thing?

Changing career is always a difficult decision. Giving up a well-paid job to start a new business is even more difficult. Many parents choose to go into childminding whilst at home with their own young children. Many more leave their existing jobs to try their hand at working for themselves. Further, a large number of people who work in private nurseries often decide to set up their own business; lacking the funds to open their own nursery, they might decide to set up a childminding business instead. Do bear in mind that although you might have experience in working with children, running a business does come with many other responsibilities.

The actual financial outlay is relatively low as far as setting up a childminding business is concerned and you may even be eligible for a grant to assist you in the purchase of essential items such as toys and equipment. However, if you are used to receiving a regular income, it can come as quite a shock if, after several months, you are still struggling to get your business venture off the ground. It is not unusual for many new businesses to struggle to make a profit in the first year or so and quite often new businesses are still making a loss after a couple of years. Childminding is no exception. Despite the fact that money may not come rolling in thick and fast at the start you will still need to find the money to pay for insurance, advertising and marketing and toys and equipment.

If you are currently working in another profession and are about to hand in your notice to set up your childminding business, I would advise holding off until you have been registered as a childminder, have completed the compulsory training and have guaranteed customers waiting for a place. There is nothing stopping you from setting up your business and advertising your vacancies whilst you are working. This will prevent you from having to sit tight for several months waiting for customers whilst you struggle along surviving on bread and water!

Whether or not you are actually doing the right thing by setting up a childminding business from home is something no one can answer but you. Most certainly you will need to enjoy being with young children and have the ability to satisfy their needs and requirements. You will need to have a business head on your shoulders and you will need to be 110 per cent committed to your venture.

Coping with the demands of working from home

Working from home does have its advantages. First, you will escape the rush hour traffic and avoid having to sit for an hour nose to tail with a million other vehicles all going in your direction. Second, you will save on travelling expenses. Third, you will be at home with your own children. The disadvantages depend on the sort of person you are and your own family circumstances.

The money and time you save by not having to travel into work will quickly be superseded by the cost of having your suite and carpets regularly cleaned and the extra amount of housework you will be required to do after entertaining a bunch of rowdy children all day. Being at home with your own children may sound a good idea initially but some parents will be driven mad when faced with the very real prospect of not being able to escape their offspring! Although many parents return to work because finances dictate there are a great deal of others who do so because they enjoy their careers and feel they respond better as a parent when they have some time away from their children. Childminders are human too. We are not robots and sometimes we need some space away from home to spend some time enjoying adult company and sensible conversation. This rarely happens in a childminding household so try to ensure you make some time for it!

Working from home also demands a huge amount of commitment on a daily basis. You will be inviting people into your house every day and it is absolutely paramount that your house stands up to the scrutiny which this will entail. Be prepared for some worn muddy carpets, grubby finger marks, chipped paint and empty food cupboards. Many children will show very little respect for your home. I shudder when I think of the times my sofas have been used as trampolines and how children have displayed acrobatic routines in their parent's arms that even Olga Korbut would be proud of, arms flying as I frantically try to catch my light fitting before it smashes to the floor! I have heard stories from childminders who have had their cars kicked by unruly children, their expensive hi-fi systems broken and their televisions smeared with jam. It's all part of the job isn't it? Well, no it isn't – you wouldn't let your child walk into a classroom and wreck it, so neither is it really acceptable to walk into a childminder's home and show absolutely no respect! Sadly though, it can happen.

Knowing exactly how to deal with such things is the hard part! It is important that you value the things which are important to you, your family, your home and your possessions, and that you recognize your strengths and weaknesses. This does not mean that you have an unrealistic inflated view of things but that you recognize your good points and feel confident protecting people and things of value to you.

Also remember, not only does childminding require a great deal in the way of commitment from *you*, but it also requires full commitment from your *family*. Without their help and support your business will suffer. As a childminder you will probably be running your business from your own living spaces. If you are very fortunate you may have a separate playroom from which you can run your business – however the majority of childminders are not so lucky, and it is essential that you have the backing of your family as it is of course their living space too. It won't just be your privacy which is invaded every time a child and their parent walk into your home, but every member of your family will be affected in some way or another and they will need to be committed to your business venture in much the same way as you are. It may be that your own children become firm friends with the children you care for and this could be the start of wonderful, long-term friendships, but consider how things may get difficult if the children do not get on. How will you cope if your own children have difficulty sharing their toys and, more importantly, their mum with other children? Some children cope admirably in these circumstances whilst others struggle immensely. Much will depend on the age of your own children and those whom you care for and you should bear all these things in mind when deciding how many children you wish to care for and what ages.

Talk to each and every member of your family. Ask for everyone's opinion. Take their concerns into account and work things through *together*. Only if each member of the family feels that their opinions and preferences have been taken into account can you successfully come to a conclusion that will work for everyone. Never ignore niggling doubts hoping they will go away as usually they don't. In fact these niggling doubts usually multiply at an alarming rate and threaten to engulf the entire venture, if not dealt with successfully from the start.

Once you have agreed to provide care for a child and signed a contract you should feel *committed* to them. By signing a contract with a child's parent you have agreed to commit yourself to a legally binding agreement and you should keep to your side of this agreement as much as possible.

Pacing yourself

We have looked at the pitfalls of handing in your notice before your business is up and running and the risk you take of not having a decent income for a while but what happens if you are lucky or unlucky enough to experience the flip side of the coin? What if customers are queuing at your gate and banging down your door in desperation for a place for their child? Fantastic! I hear you say, wringing your hands together with pound signs glinting in your eyes. Your business is a success! Don't be too hasty is the advice I will give you in this case. We all know the saying 'don't try running before you can walk' and this has never been truer than in the case of setting up a childminding business!

You can never have any idea of what a job actually entails until you start doing it. In the case of childminding, this is quite simply because no two families are alike and the childcare required for one child will be very different from that required for another. Enrol on all the courses available, read all the books that have ever been written and talk to as many parents as you can but nothing will prepare you better than actually giving the job a go, so pace yourself!

Receiving an enquiry is not the same as securing custom and you may be lulled into a false sense of security if, at first, you are inundated with enquiries. Don't be fooled into thinking everyone who makes an enquiry is a serious contender for your business. Some people like to look at the competition on offer and compare prices and facilities, others are simply nosey and want to know what you are up to!

Take your time and choose wisely. Don't accept business from the first person who crosses your threshold. You have to be as certain as can be that you can work with them. You need to satisfy yourself that the parents and children you welcome into your home every day are the sort of people you wish to befriend and offer a service to. You need to be sure that these parents share your own views of childcare as much as possible. You need to be certain that they will keep their side of the contract, pay you on time every time and provide you with the necessary items you require to carry out your duties to the best of your ability.

There is no foolproof way of knowing that the parents who come to you will not, sometime down the line, cause you problems. After over 13 years in the job I am still surprised at how quickly parents can turn on you if things aren't going their way or if they have had a bad day at work! My advice is to try as much as possible to ignore this kind of behaviour. Continue to be professional and carry out your duties to the best of your ability.

How you pace yourself will depend on a number of things:

1   How many childcare places you have available

2   How many children of your own you have

3   The ages of your own children

4   Whether you work with another childminder or an assistant.

If you are registered to care for three children under the age of five and you already have a three-year-old and a six-month-old baby of your own then you will only have one day care place to fill. Most childminders can only provide care for one baby under the age of 12 months but exceptions are made in some circumstances. However I would advise anyone to think carefully about requesting to care for more than one baby. Babies are very demanding with sleep and feeding routines and you may find yourself doing very little other than changing nappies and making up bottles. Your own three-year-old may suffer and you will quickly become exhausted and worn down. Think carefully whom your ideal child would be. Perhaps another three-year-old child as a friend for your own child would be the ideal answer. However there is no guarantee that you will get enquiries from parents with children of this age and if you are lucky enough to get an enquiry you or your child may not feel that they are suitable.

It is very tempting, when setting up a new business, to take *any* customer who may come knocking on your door. This is a bad idea. For one thing never appear desperate to potential customers. Promising everything in return for a couple of quid will not appear professional and will not get your business off to a good start. You may even find yourself being taken advantage of.

Allowing yourself to be manipulated will make you end up feeling like a 'jack of all trades and master of none'. You are not a low-paid babysitter, you are a qualified childminder providing a professional service.

Once a placement has begun and contracts have been signed you have to remember that you have an obligation to that family. This is why you should think carefully before accepting a placement. Are the days and hours what you are looking for? Filling all your vacancies immediately leaves little room for manoeuvre and, if you do find the going tough, you risk letting one or more of the families down, which is not good for the children or for your business. Childminders who are not reliable will quickly get a name for themselves and will be avoided like the plague. You are far better to start off slowly. Fill one place and see how you get on. If you cope well and feel that you would like to take on more children then now is the time to do so.

Although filling every vacancy you have every day makes good financial sense it will be extremely exhausting. Decide from the outset if you want to work part time or full time and stick to your decision. Think about how you would feel if you only had one vacancy and you took on a child for two days per week when, a couple of weeks later, you got a request for a full-time place. Ideally you would like the full-time placement as five days' pay is preferable to two. But how can you go back on your word to the first parent?

Believing in yourself and your ability to succeed

For any business to succeed you have to believe in yourself and the service you provide and childminding is no exception. If you are experiencing a lack of customers, don't let it get you down. Think of new ways of advertising and marketing, and never give up.

If you give yourself and your business time to adapt you will get customers – unless you live at the top of Ben Nevis when perhaps the only things to come wandering around your home are white and woolly! I have yet to meet a childminder who, after having registered, has not filled at least one of their places within six months. They may not have filled all of their vacancies and are very likely to be working part time after such a relatively short space of time but, as with most businesses, getting the first customer is usually the most difficult. Word of mouth is *the* most important way of securing business for childminders. Parents like to feel that they are leaving their children with someone who is trustworthy and confident and what better advertisement than an existing parent singing your praises?

Your commitment to childminding should never stop at simply pleasing parents although this is of course an important part of the job. You should also be committed to the children, providing them with the best care you possibly can, all day, every day. You should ensure that each child in your care has their age, stage of development, culture, beliefs and preferences considered and that each child is treated as an individual.

You commitment should also extend to training. Completing an introductory course and attending first-aid training may be compulsory but this does not mean that you should look at this as the only training necessary for the job. Childminders should show professionalism at all times and, in order to keep abreast of the many changes in childcare practice and to remain a reflective practitioner, it will be necessary for you to show a commitment to training. Keep yourself up to date with the training offered by your local authority and enrol on courses periodically to refresh your knowledge of childcare procedures and make your business stand out from the crowd.

5
Taking charge of your first child

So here you are, registration certificate proudly framed and displayed on your dining room wall, and surrounded by enough toys and equipment to give the Early Learning Centre a run for their money! You have a fireguard fitted, safety gates, socket covers, a fridge lock, window locks and drawer locks. Your home resembles Fort Knox and you need a crowbar to open the washing machine – but safety *is* paramount when childminding. All you need now are some children! You sit patiently by the telephone willing it to ring. When it does it ends up being a double-glazing salesman and your frustration reaches an all-time high.

What exactly are customers looking for?

It would be good to be able to answer this question with features like good qualifications, a fun and educational environment, good quality resources etc. but the simple truth of the matter is that parents, if honest, are more likely to rate the following factors as the most influential when making their decision about childcare:

- Reliability – no parent wants a childminder who is unreliable and who will let them down at a minute's notice when they need to go to work.

- Cost – no amount of qualifications or resources will allow you to charge excessive rates for your service. Often parents' ability to pay is influenced by their own earning power and your service must reflect value for money if you hope to fill your places.

- Trustworthiness – the parents need to know that they can trust you and be certain that their child will be safe in your care.

- Location – the proximity of your setting to the home of the child is a big deciding factor. Parents rarely want to travel great distances for childcare.

Other factors, such as the facilities you have to offer, your experience in caring for children and your qualifications, will be considered but do not usually take precedence over the points mentioned above. Parents do however take notice of how approachable you are. A gruff, stern childminder will not appeal to parents or children!

Finding customers

You have placed neatly typed, well-presented notices in your local shop windows and on the school's notice board. You have trudged for miles around the new housing development posting leaflets through the letter boxes hoping that any new families moving into the area may require the services of a good childminder and you have registered your details with the Children's Information Service, so why haven't you got any customers? Patience, as I have said before, is a virtue and this is one time when you are simply going to have to be patient!

There is no real set pattern for enquiries in this business. Carpet fitters and furniture manufacturers always appear to have a mad rush just before Christmas when everyone wants new furniture in time for the festive season, and then a lull in the summer when most people are away on holiday. Childminding, however, is simply not that cut and dried, because women are having babies

all the time! You may get an influx of enquiries through the
summer months from parents whose children are due to start
school in September but, other than this, there is no real pattern
to childcare enquiries.

Business will come to you but at what rate it is impossible to
predict. Bar poaching custom from rivals – which will only result
in you losing friends, or reducing your fees dramatically to try to
lure customers – which in turn will only result in you running
your business at a loss, you will have to be patient and sit things
out.

You could ask around your local area and speak to other
childminders to get a 'feel' for the general number of enquiries
they are receiving and, if they haven't got any vacancies
themselves, they may even be willing to put your name forward to
any prospective customers who come knocking on their door.
However competition can be fierce and sometimes other
childminders are reluctant to help, especially if business is quiet
for them also. So the simple answer is to sit tight and ride out the
quiet times. This is obviously much easier if you are still working
and earning a living – it is a lot harder and much more deflating if
the bills are piling up and you can see no light at the end of the
tunnel. Many childminders I know have taken temporary jobs
whilst waiting for business to generate and of course this is
another way of meeting new people and getting your name around
whilst earning money at the same time.

Word of mouth is one of the most successful ways of securing
business and this is why the first customer is always the hardest to
find. No parent who is already using your service is going to talk
detrimentally about your ability to look after children and, should
any of their friends and acquaintances be looking for childcare,
they are sure to put your name forward.

Others ways of generating business that you may like to consider are:

1. Stick a poster in the window of your car. You will be advertising your service whilst driving around. Best of all, this kind of advertising is free!

2. Get your name around by attending parent and toddler sessions, PTA meetings etc. It is usually quite easy to drop into conversation what you do for a living and most parents are keen to glean as much information from new recruits as possible.

3. Consider advertising your service in newsletters such as your local school or support groups.

4. Approach local businesses in your area and enquire about the possibility of putting an advert on their notice board advertising your childcare service.

5. The internet is a good way of advertising your business and many childminders now have their own websites.

6. Think about having some business cards printed, or enquire whether your local authority has any pre-printed for you to just fill in your details. Business cards are very useful to hand out when you are attending support groups etc. Ask whether you can leave a few cards in prominent places such as your local GP's surgery, dentist's waiting room etc.

When the telephone finally rings you will inevitably be unprepared. After sitting for weeks on end staring at a silent telephone and practising your opening speech to anyone within earshot, you can be almost certain that when that first enquiry does come you will either be out or chewing on a toffee!

Assuming you are chewing on a toffee, spit the offending sweet into your hand and frantically try to regain your composure! This telephone call is *very* important. This is your chance to sell yourself. If the parent does not feel that you are professional or you appear flustered and unsure of yourself they will not be impressed. If they are not impressed they will not make an appointment to see you and, of course, if they do not come to see you, you will not secure any business. Make sure you focus on all the positive things you have to offer whilst answering the parent's questions truthfully. Avoid letting them 'think about it'. Try to make a secure appointment with them whilst you have their attention. After all they want a childminder, they have contacted you, you are a childminder and you *want* business!

You put the telephone down, head spinning but feeling rather smug and elated by the fact that you have had your first enquiry. The parent is calling to see you in an hour's time. You frantically look around your house. The same house which has been in pristine condition for the past four months waiting for this very moment but which now looks like a nuclear fall out shelter! The safety features which would have impressed just about anyone have been removed in frustration after you had failed on many occasions to open the fridge door because of the child lock. You run around with the vacuum cleaner, plumping cushions as you go along and drag a brush through your hair. You sit nervously in a hastily tidied lounge surrounded with an impressive array of new toys and wait for the potential customer to arrive.

The arranged appointment time comes and goes. The knock on the door you are anticipating becomes a distant hope and you begin to dissect the conversation you had on the telephone earlier. What did you say? Where did you go wrong? How have you put them off? Just then the knock on the door comes and you are momentarily glued to your seat. Pulse racing, head spinning, you yank open the door expecting, well not quite sure what you are expecting, and you meet eye to eye with a parent holding hands with their child.

First impressions

First impressions work both ways. An interview is an important way for the parent to gain an insight into the kind of service you provide and it is equally important for you, the childminder, to ascertain whether this is the kind of family you wish to work with.

When meeting a prospective customer it is important to remember that you are aiming to try to persuade them that your childminding service is the best on offer in your area. Avoid putting competitors down in order to secure business as this smacks of desperation. Remember that not all parents will be aware of how a childminding service works and, if they are new to the childcare search, it may be a good idea for you to guide them through the process and explain the procedure for finding and registering with a childminder. The more information a parent has the better equipped they will be at deciding exactly what they want, thus preventing them from changing their minds later on down the line. By being helpful and informative, but not pushy and desperate, you will go a long way in securing business.

Interviews get easier with practice but it is probably true to say that the initial apprehension never really subsides. If you understand the importance of first impressions then you will inevitably become a little nervous when meeting parents for the first time. You want to make a good impression but understand that trying too hard can be off-putting. There is a fine line between being blasé and becoming a push-over and you need to tread carefully in order to give a professional impression.

Shaking hands, you usher the mother and child into your living room and then the fun really begins! The angelic-looking child is really the devil incarnate. Picking up your brand new toys he systematically pulls each one apart and tells his mother that the toys here 'suck'. You try to ignore the child and give your attention to the mother who proceeds to tell you exactly what she expects in the way of care for her child. She tells you when she is going on holiday and expects you to go at the same time, she tells you the hours she wants and even how much she is willing to pay, leaving you no chance to get a word in edgeways.

One thing you should always remember is that you should *never* let a parent dictate your working terms. This is *your* business. *You* set the days, times and fees and then it is for the parent to decide whether the service you provide is suitable for them. Remember you will not have just one family to keep happy. Eventually, when your business takes off, you could well have children from several families to care for and if each one lays down the law and tells you what they want it will be impossible for you to carry out your duties.

Even at the interview stage if a child or parent is saying something or acting in a way that you do not approve of then say so. Remember this is your home and you have a right to respect. Ask 'Damien' to stop breaking your toys and suggest that he looks at a book if he isn't impressed with the toy collection you have. Invite him to tell you which kinds of toy he enjoys playing with and let him know if these are the kinds of thing you could supply. However don't be surprised if he says a submachine gun or a rocket launcher!

At the end of the interview – if you haven't thrown the child and parent out before that stage – then you must *both* decide if this is a working relationship you would be happy with. Invite the parent to go away and think about things and suggest that they look at other providers in order that they are certain in their own minds that the service you provide is actually what they want. That way you can be sure if they do come back to you it is because they genuinely think the service you are offering is the one they require. Avoid putting parents on the spot and getting them to sign there are then. Avoiding rushing things not only gives them the chance to think things through at their own pace, but it also gives you the chance to recap on the interview and deal with any issues which may have come to light.

Some people would argue that by allowing a parent to leave without getting them to sign on the dotted line you are risking losing their business. I disagree entirely. Pressurizing a parent to sign up with you immediately reeks of desperation, and you don't want to come across as desperate, even if the bailiffs are banging on your door!

There will however be parents who simply *insist* on signing a contract there and then. You may be the last childminder they have visited on a long list and they are absolutely certain that you are the person they want to care for their child. If this is the case and the parents have looked at everything else on offer then by all means go ahead and fill out contracts if this is also what *you* want. However make sure that you are absolutely certain that this is a family you can work with before committing yourself.
Encouraging parents to look at competition not only gives them time to mull things over, it also gives you valuable time to decide whether the family are what you are looking for. This is why it is essential that you are open and honest at the interview stage. If you sign the contracts during the interview, it will not be an option to let the parent down over the telephone at a later date because you simply don't think you could work with them (you could always say you are very sorry but the vacancy is no longer available to avoid hurting their feelings), so you must be certain that you can offer what they need. If you are unsure, be honest! Explain any points which are worrying you. If little Damien is acting in a manner which you consider unacceptable then by telling him and his mother at the interview stage you will be making sure that everyone is aware of how you expect children to behave. If you allow Damien to break the toys and treat your home disrespectfully and say nothing you can't really blame him for thinking that you don't mind and will allow this kind of behaviour to continue if you are brave enough to take him on!

So your first interview didn't turn out as you had hoped. Do not despair! Pick yourself up, dust yourself down and prepare for the next one. One setback isn't the end of the world.

Learn by your mistakes. Look carefully at what went wrong – look at your own expectations again and weigh up how different these seem to be to the potential customer's own requirements. Although I do not think you should agree to things which are clearly impossible for you to provide, I do think you may need to come up with ways of compromising. Compromise is a big word in childminding. Often the childminder feels they are the only one compromising but for things to work successfully there must be give and take on both sides. Rather than refusing point blank to do something requested of you try offering alternatives in order to come up with an idea that appeals to everyone. Parents may not be happy at being told you cannot accommodate their every wish but the blow will be cushioned if you can offer alternative, reasonable compromises.

Remember if a parent doesn't choose your service don't take it to heart – it doesn't mean that you are a bad childminder or that the service you are offering is poor compared to the competition. It simply means that they have managed to find someone more suitable for their particular circumstances. Often parents will not come back to you if they have decided to go elsewhere and you may be left wondering what you have done wrong. Try not to go through things with a fine-tooth comb. It may be something as simple as the parent deciding not to return to work after all!

Being prepared

Ideally you should be prepared for enquiries at any time during your preferred working hours. You may still get parents telephoning at 10pm enquiring about vacancies but you can reasonably expect the majority of parents to telephone at respectable hours of the day. If you are still working or you are likely to be away from the telephone during the day it is essential that you get an answering machine to avoid missing vital enquiries from potential customers.

Being prepared both before you set your business up and after is an essential part of childminding. The job of caring for young children is varied and every day is different. It can be very difficult to anticipate problems but being prepared goes a long way to avoiding any pitfalls. No one expects you to live your life in a show home ready and eager to show potential customers around your spotless house with neatly arranged toys on display. I for one, as a parent, would not be impressed! Would my child be allowed to touch *anything*? Would they actually be allowed to breathe? A too perfect home can be just as off-putting as a dirty, shambolic one. You should be striving for a happy medium.

A house which is homely and welcoming, where the parents and children can feel relaxed and at ease, is the kind you should be aiming for. Above all your house must be clean! This is one area where you must be very diligent. Parents may not notice if your DVD collection is not stored in alphabetical order or your flowers are not arranged neatly in a vase but they will notice sticky finger marks on the walls, stained carpets and a dirty kitchen and they will not be impressed. Even those who are allergic to housework in their own homes and have never seen a pair of rubber gloves will not tolerate a dirty childminder. After all, you will be looking after their children, and they will not expect to have to pay you for the privilege of infecting their offspring with salmonella or dysentery.

With your house prepared to receive potential customers the only other thing left to prepare is yourself! You need to appear confident and professional. Parents will be trusting you with the care of their children and they will not be impressed if the person sat before them is a dithering wreck unable to answer the simplest of questions. Preparing yourself is a necessity and you would be well advised to practise what you will say prior to making any appointments. Try to anticipate the kinds of question parents may ask: this is not as difficult as it may appear – I am not asking you to take a crash course in telepathy! It simply means giving some thought to how you intend to run your business on a daily basis as this will enable you to answer most of the questions parents may put to you. What would *you* like to ask someone you were leaving your children with? Most parents need to be reassured that their children will be:

1   Safe

2   Happy

3   Entertained

4   Valued

5   Fed and watered!

Parents may arrive at your house armed with a list of questions as long as your arm and you may wonder how on earth you will be able to answer them all. The most important thing to remember is to be yourself, be honest and talk about the positive aspects of your business.

If parents make a request for something you feel you are unable or unwilling to do then it is important, at this stage, that you say so. It is unfair and unprofessional to promise something that you later find you cannot carry out. Securing business in this manner is not the way to go about things and you risk ruining your reputation before your business has even got off the ground if you mess parents around by allowing them to believe you can offer them something which you cannot.

Some of the more common questions parents will ask you during an interview are listed below. Aim to have an answer for each prior to the interview.

Parents will probably ask you:

1   How many days and hours you are available

2   How much you charge

3   How many children you are registered to care for

4   How many children you are currently caring for and their ages

5   How long you have been childminding and how much experience you have

6   How many weeks holiday per annum you take

7   When these holidays are usually taken

8   Whether you work unsocial hours or weekends (necessary for parents who work shift patterns, for example, police officers, doctors, nurses etc.)

9   Which schools, nurseries and playgroups you service

10 Which areas of your house the children have access to

11 Whether you attend toddler groups or take the children on outings

12 How much experience you have in caring for babies

13 What activities you provide

14 What meals you provide

15 Details of your usual daily routine.

Organizing your home and family life

When you initially sat down to discuss your ideas for setting up a childminding business from home it is probably true to say that your partner and children liked the idea – your partner because of the added income, your children because of the potential to have friends round to play all day every day! However it is probably also true to say that neither your partner nor your children will have given the idea much *serious* thought. Working from home is difficult and I would be lying if I said that it does not cause problems from time to time. You will often find yourself being pulled in several directions: trying to keep your partner happy, your children happy, your childminded children happy, their parents happy and bottom of the list, yourself happy! It is a juggling act and only the most organized of childminders pass the test.

Childminding is a family venture in that everyone must be in agreement on the rules and understand the implications that working long hours from home can bring.

Your partner may:

1   Resent sharing his home with others

2   Be less tolerant of children than you are

3   Be unhappy with the noise

4   Dislike the mess made by young children

5   Resent not being able to do the things he would like to do whilst you are childminding, for example, smoking

6   Find it hard having children in the house when he comes home from work

7   Find it difficult having children in the house if he works shift patterns. How would you keep a crying baby and boisterous children quiet if your partner worked night shifts and needed to sleep during the day?

Your children may:

1   Not get on with the children you care for

2   Resent the time you give to other children

3   Resent having to share their home and toys with other children every day

4   Find it difficult to do their homework with young children in the house, particularly if they are older and need to study for exams

5   Get upset if their toys get broken.

All these issues must be addressed before you continue with your plans to set up a childminding business. Ignoring potential problems will not make them go away. However, being prepared for them will make things a lot easier. Other questions you may need to ask yourself are:

1   How would you feel if parents walked into your home in the morning without knocking?

2   How would you feel about being on call over and above your standard working hours? Parents may telephone you late on Sunday evening to ask you how much lunch money their child will need to take to school the next day or whether they have left their swimming bag in your kitchen, *if* you allow them to.

3   How would you feel about being expected to work with little or no notice?

By making sure that your own home and family life are well organized you will be well on the way to ensuring a smooth-running, successful business. You will need to get all of your family members on board and make sure that they are all aware of their responsibilities and that they promise to keep to their side of the bargain. No one is saying that your seven-year-old should take responsibility for cooking the family's evening meal and ironing the clothes but allocating them simple jobs like keeping their rooms tidy and helping to clear the table after dinner all help to make your job that little bit easier. Your partner may be used to coming home from work at the end of the day and sitting in front of the television until his evening meal is served. This will quickly become a distant dream when you start childminding! He is more likely to come home to a house full of tired whinging children and have to get on with peeling the vegetables if he wants to be fed. Rest assured your partner will not die from pulling his weight, in fact, he may even realize just how difficult keeping a job and family together really is and he may even be more understanding when you tell him you are exhausted at 9pm!

6

Working in partnership with parents

Parents are the most important and influential people in their children's lives and it is important to respect this relationship at all times. As a childminder your role is to provide quality childcare in accordance with the preferences of the parents. Compromises may need to be made along the way in order to accommodate all of the children in your care, but essentially you should be looking to work with each child's parents in order to provide the best care possible.

Family structures

Families come in all shapes and sizes and it is probably true to say that the 'traditional' family consisting of a mother and father living together with their children is in decline.

The following table shows the different family structures.

Table 6.1

Family Structure	Description
The 'average' or 'nuclear' family	Both parents living in the same house with their children.
The 'reconstituted' family	This type of family structure consists of one natural parent and one step-parent living with the children.
The 'single' or 'one-parent' family	This is when one parent lives on their own with the children. This type of family structure may come about as a result of divorce, death, personal choice or because of the breakdown of a relationship.
The 'adoptive' family	This is when the child is living with adults who are not their natural parents. The child may be unaware that they have been adopted and therefore give the impression that they are part of a nuclear or extended family.
The 'foster' family	This is when a child is placed with adults who are not their natural parents for varying lengths of time. This may be because of family or child protection issues.
The 'gay' or 'lesbian' family	This type of family structure comes about when a child is living with one natural parent who has a partner of the same sex. This may also occur when a child is adopted.
The 'extended' family	This type of family structure was traditional in the UK for many centuries and is still very common in many parts of the world. Many members of the same family including the parents, children, grandparents, aunts and uncles live in close proximity to one another, sometimes in the same house and often share the childcare duties.
The 'communal' family	This is where a number of families, who are unrelated, live together in the same house effectively forming an extended family for the children.

Understanding parents' feelings

When parents leave their children with you they may experience a wide range of feelings, particularly if they are returning to work for the first time since having their baby. It is important that you consider these feelings and make allowances, where possible, for the effects that these feelings may have on the way the parents communicate with you and behave towards you.

Parents may feel:

- Guilty – This is a very common experience for many parents when they return to work. They may feel guilty at *having* to leave their child or guilty for *wanting* to leave them. Either way guilt is a very powerful emotion and needs to be acknowledged.

- Jealousy – Many parents feel jealous towards their child's carer, particularly if they develop a close bond. It is important that you reassure the parents and never try to take their place in their child's affections. Share information with the parents about what you have been doing with their child in order to involve them as much as possible in their day to day care. Parents may be jealous of the fact that you can stay at home with your own children whilst still earning a living.

- Frustration – Another very powerful emotion which is often difficult to control. Parents may become frustrated for any number of reasons. Their child may be difficult for them to manage and the stress of having to hold down a job and be a parent often proves hard for some parents. They may be frustrated at having to leave their child and resent missing out on spending time with them and watching them grow and develop. Once again, you can make this easier by sharing the day's events with them and involving them as much as possible in their child's daily care.

- Anger – Parents may become angry at having to leave their child in order to return to work. Although it must be said that some parents want to return to work and thrive on the mixture of work and family life by finding a happy balance, many others have to go back to work, perhaps for financial reasons, and resent the time spent away from their children enormously.

- Upset – Whereas some parents become angry at having to leave their child, others may become upset. New mothers returning to work will have mixed emotions about the whole 'return to work' scenario and their hormones and emotions may well be riding high following the recent birth of their child. Quite often mothers who have been out of the workplace for some time may suffer from anxiety and lack confidence.

Parents come in all shapes and sizes; there is no such thing as an 'average' parent. Their beliefs, values and ideas will vary enormously. Very broadly speaking, most parents will fall into one of the following categories.

The involved parents

Are 'involved parents' a childminder's dream or a childminder's nightmare? These types of parent are likely to want to know absolutely everything their child has been doing whilst in your care. They will have a long list of 'preferences' and will take an active interest in everything you tell them. They may appear supportive, understanding, considerate and willing to accept that their child is not perfect – basically a childminder's dream!

On the other hand involved parents may be defensive to the extreme, believing that their child is an angel who can do no wrong. Problems will inevitably occur here if you need to discuss any issues concerning the child with their parents. You will be met with disbelief and utter horror from parents who genuinely believe their daughter is simply incapable of being mean, rude or spiteful. 'She's never rude to us, is she Jeffrey?' the mother will state whilst her eight-year-old daughter sits slouching in the chair, drumming her fingers and smirking all over her face.

These types of parent, though involved, will wash their hands of this sort of issue and simply put it down to the fact that you have failed to interact successfully.

Other 'involved parents' need constant reassurance from you. They will expect you to tell them how clever their child is and how advanced they are in comparison to other children (even though the child is only three months old and spends his days gurgling at the ceiling and being sick down your blouse!). You may try, albeit unsuccessfully, to explain that it is not advisable to 'compare' children as they all develop at different speeds, but your protestations will almost certainly fall on deaf ears as they continue to indulge their beliefs that their child is superior to all others.

Some parents will enrol their child in every class – hoping their three-year-old will also pick up French and Spanish before they've even grasped the English language! They might also expect *you* to help them with the language lessons and might not fully appreciate that you will have other children to look after and might not have enough time.

Occasionally you might come across parents who used to be childminders themselves who will always have advice for you – you might feel that whatever you say, this parent is convinced that they can do your job better and more efficiently. Again, remember first and foremost to be confident in your own abilities and take on/ignore such guidance as you prefer (you may find it helpful to learn from their experiences; you may find it a hindrance!). It could be the case that the profession and training have changed considerably since they were childminding.

Involved parents as you can see then are variable. Some make our jobs easy, some make it nigh on impossible. As mentioned, all parents are individual and have their own unique ways. It is important to remember that their relationship with their child is the most important and that though you might have different approaches to parenthood, you must always bear in mind that parents are the most important and influential people in a child's life. Priority should be given to developing a good working relationship with parents of children in your care. Establish the way you prefer to run your home and business (see Chapter 10 for advice on writing policies) and feel comfortable and confident in finding the best way to compromise if needed to maintain this positive relationship, no matter what the situation might be. Should you feel that it is important to talk to a parent find a good time to do so for you both and don't be shy of sharing with the parents your routine and methods of caring for, and meeting the needs of, *all* the children in your care. It is always a good idea to spend time initially explaining your policies and procedures to parents so that they are aware of how you run your business, what they can expect from you and what, in turn, you will expect from them.

The unavailable parents

You may find that there are some parents whom you will never see. Their family and friends will drop their child off at your house at the beginning of each day and collect them again at the end; every telephone call you make or note you send home will be met with silence; and your payments might be made directly into your bank account. There may be any number of reasons for this. The parents might be very busy, they might work shift patterns or unsocial hours, or they might simply shy away from any kind of contact preferring to keep their distance. In theory this makes for a rather peaceful life for the childminder – it sure beats a pushy parent on your door step every day! However, the problems with unavailable parents begin to surface if you have a reason for needing to contact them. This could be with regard to concerns over the child's behaviour, or general day to day issues, or contract problems. The parents who are difficult to contact on a normal day are often even less likely to respond if there is a problem.

You could try making an appointment for them to call and see you, but this can of course only be done if you manage to contact them at all, and then there might also be times when such an appointment is forgotten or unavoidably broken at the last minute. If you suggest calling at their home you might be met with drawn curtains and a locked door.

To ensure that you always have contact with the parents of children in your care I would advise that from the outset you regularly talk about who will be dropping off and collecting the child you are caring for, and say how important it is, for a number of reasons, to see the parent once a week/fortnight. Always make sure that you know the person who has been sent to collect a child from your setting and if you are in any doubt whatsoever *never* hand a child over without first verifying who they are.

It might be useful to issue parents with a 'diary' which you can both use to write important information in and use this to reiterate how important it is to speak face to face with them periodically. Let parents know that you are available to speak to them outside your usual working hours if necessary.

The busy parents

Invariably parents are busy – or can be at the times you will see them, as they are rushing to drop their children off on the way to work, or are keen to get home as they pick their children up after a long day. Some will forget the nappies, the formula milk, the teething gel, worst of all your money! This is not unusual and the key thing is that as a childminder you are equipped and ready to begin your day's work – with all the teething gel you need! It is also important never to underestimate the power of a parent's love for their child, however their time is spent and however they choose to bring them up.

The 'you deal with it' parents

Some parents are happy for you to deal with everyday problems and prefer you not to raise inconsequential matters – but, heaven forbid you dealing with a situation in a way that they are not happy with – they will be down on you like a ton of bricks! They may let you believe that you have a long leash when it comes to caring for their offspring but believe me this leash will hang you if you are not careful.

Never deal with any situations without informing the parents. Things will come back to haunt you if you are not honest and open about issues and how you have dealt with them.

The difficult parents

No matter what you do, how you do it, what you give or how little you charge, difficult parents will *rarely* be satisfied all of the time. The four-course gourmet lunch you cooked, though appealing and healthy, might be improved if you offer mashed potatoes next time instead of new potatoes as 'these are easier for Harriet to digest'.

They might expect you to spend hours helping their child with their homework. (The worst part of this is when, after spending an hour a day every day helping the child to learn their spellings, they end up getting seven out of ten during the test at the end of the week. Difficult parents won't blame their child for not getting full marks, they will blame you, as you obviously haven't put in sufficient work to ensure that they get ten out of ten!)

Difficult parents will read between the lines when it comes to contracts and, no matter how foolproof you think your contract is, they will find something they can twist to their advantage. They will argue your fees and get you to reduce these even if it means they only save 20p a week. You will of course be faced with this kind of problem every time you increase your fees and, if you are not careful, you will end up reducing the fee rather than increasing it just to get the parents off your back! Putting your fees up by an extortionate amount in the vain hope that the parents will refuse to pay and find another childminder is not the answer. Yes, they will refuse to pay but they don't give up easily and will most definitely fight you tooth and nail until they win and secure another year's contract at a greatly reduced price. I am not trying to say that childminders are feeble and unable to stand up for themselves in this kind of situation, merely that difficult parents are just that, 'difficult', and confidently adept at getting their own way!

Remember again that the priority is that you are able to maintain a good working relationship with the parents of children in your care. Be confident in the way you run your business, and firm and fair, striking a balance between compromising when it is important to, yet never to the detriment of your business. All cases are individual but everything gets a little easier with experience!

The 'unable to cope' parents

Some parents are submissive, often bullied by their own children. Whilst trying to befriend their offspring they have lost their way with parental control. These parents will look to you for help, advice and reassurance, and you might find this an easy situation to handle; alternatively you might find it draining and exhausting if their dependence on you becomes a little too much (phone calls at the weekend!).

Again everyone is individual. As long as you go into situations with open eyes you should find a good way of handling such cases. Try to give as much help and advice as you can and remember that usually the difficult stages of parenting pass fairly quickly (it may be that a new mum is exhausted through lack of sleep, for example, and is feeling low and in need of reassurance). If, however, the parent is encroaching excessively on your time and this is affecting your own family life then you may have to tactfully explain things to them.

To summarize, whichever type of parents you may find yourself working with, it is always worth bearing in mind that *all* parents want the best for their children. Their understandings of 'the best' may differ considerably but the simple fact is that parents are usually happy if their children are happy. The lives of the parents and the childminders will run smoothly if the children enjoy the time they spend in the childminding setting; therefore, although it is important to try to please parents, it is more important to provide for the children's needs. It is in fact often much easier to keep children happy than it is their parents (and I don't mean bribing them with sweets). Whereas parents may come with a complete agenda of things they wish you to provide, children, on the other hand, usually require:

1   A safe, happy environment

2   Love and understanding

3   Attention

4   Stimulation and entertainment

5   Nourishment.

If these basic needs are met, children are usually responsive and undemanding – unlike many parents!

It is also important to remember that, where there are many different types of family and parenting styles, there are also many different forms of childcare and, although you personally may not be able to offer suitable childcare for one particular family, this does not mean that another childminder will have the same difficulty. Working in partnership with parents means recognizing the things you cannot do as well as those you can and it is important that you admit if something is difficult for you rather than pretend to go along with things just to please the parent.

Continuity of care is essential for children and you therefore need to be certain that you can work in partnership with the parents of the children you care for in order for the children to reach their full potential and enjoy their time with you. Although parents are the first educators of their children, childcare is a two-way process that requires both the parents and the practitioner to exchange information regularly, seek each other's opinions and share details of progress and achievement. It will be much easier for you to do this if you genuinely *like* the people you provide a service for and this is one of the important reasons for carrying out an interview. You should be able to tell at this stage whether you find the parents approachable and easy to talk to or you anticipate problems. The former is a good feeling to have, and the latter should be avoided unless you feel able to work things through.

Remember that parents can and sometimes do change their attitudes. Whereas they might have appeared to be amiable at the interview, once they have secured a contract with you, they may change considerably and become demanding and uncooperative. This is why it is necessary to have a good contract and, provided you stick to your side of any agreement, the parent should have no cause for complaint. Settling-in periods are useful for this type of situation, and if a parent tries to drastically change the initial agreement they have with you, you will be able to exercise your right to end the contract during the settling-in period. We will look at this in more detail in Chapter 9.

7
Daily routines

Childminders need to be proficient in planning. In order for your day to run smoothly and for you to fulfil your obligations successfully you will need to plan your day with military precision. You need to know where you have to be at set times of the day and be able to anticipate how long it will take for you to make certain journeys, for example, taking children to school. The school may only be a ten-minute drive away but this length of time can easily double or even treble if the weather is bad or the traffic is heavy. Before going into the different events you will probably sample on a daily basis whilst running your childminding business, I am going to take you through a typical daily routine to show you how something apparently simple and easy to follow can easily become unstuck and cause you a massive headache if you do not plan things well.

A typical daily routine

Mornings are usually the busiest times in a childminder's routine not least because of everyone coming and going, but because you will usually have to be at school for a set time making it necessary for things to run smoothly if children are to avoid being late, which is of course paramount.

Despite the hectic morning rush, it is possible to ensure that children get to school on time having eaten a good breakfast and done their homework without it resulting in you going mad!

Practice makes perfect and if you plan and implen.
and change this whenever necessary, you will be able
work out of the morning routine.

Drop offs

A typical day in the life of a childminder usually begins at around
6am when the alarm clock rings. Most childminders start their
working day at around 7.30am but experience has taught me that
this is not always early enough and, unless you want to greet
children and parents in your dressing gown (so unprofessional)
you should try to allow yourself plenty of time and aim to be ready
to receive customers at least 15 minutes before you are expecting
them.

Understandably, parents are often rushed at drop-off time and will
give little thought to the childminder. You will of course have a
plan in place for when everyone is due to arrive, but it is not
uncommon for parents who have been awake for several hours
with a crying baby, and are ready an hour before their usual time,
to see no reason why you shouldn't be wide awake and ready to
start work either and they will drop their child off in the hope that
they can make an 'early start' in the office, 'miss the traffic' or
simply find something better to do than console a crying baby!
You could try charging more for early drop offs but this rarely
works as the parent will invariably say 'I knew you wouldn't mind
– you're a star!', making you feel valued for all of ten seconds
before the baby starts screaming again.

The hour or so before school in the morning is invariably manic.
Children will arrive at various times usually tired after being
woken early so their parents can go to work, hungry because they
will not have had breakfast and miserable because they don't want
to go to school.

On top of serving breakfast you will invariably get the parent who requests that little Jimmy is tested on his spellings before setting off to school to make sure he gets full marks again this week (if he doesn't it will of course be your fault so test him you do!). Occasionally you will get a baby arriving in his pyjamas with the sorry apology of the parent not having had time to dress their child! (This might not be as bad if they themselves were dishevelled, but not if they have make-up on that looks like it has been applied by a professional and perfectly groomed hair!) Another job to do before the school run. So be prepared for the odd surprise at this time of the morning – wherever possible try to ensure there is plenty of time built into your daily routine for such scenarios!

Early morning drop offs are of course made worse if the child is new or clingy and finds it difficult to separate from their parent. This kind of problem can be overcome if you think ahead and prepare suitable activities that you know the child enjoys in order to take their minds off their parent's departure. Planning ahead in this way will inevitably make things easier for you!

Another good tip is always to allow an extra five minutes before you need to leave the house, for visits to the toilet and putting on coats and shoes. When the time comes to leave for school, help the children put their coats and shoes on and strap the little ones into the double buggy. I always walk to school with the children. Parking at most schools is a nightmare and it is also a good opportunity to get some exercise in for us all! Sometimes it will be cold and wet, but with the correct outdoor clothing there is no reason why children can't enjoy the outdoors whatever the weather and you will find that most children actually enjoy the walk. (There will of course always be the odd child who hates walking and who drags their feet and moans every step of the way!)

Breakfast

Getting a healthy breakfast down some children is a monumental task and you are left in no doubt why the parents leave this feat to you! 'I'm not hungry, I'll have something later' they will moan. You try to tempt them with anything you can, stopping short of chocolate cream cake for fear that this will then become a morning ritual!

This problem can be overcome by making sure that you are aware of what every child in your care likes to eat. Once you know their preferences you will be able to stock your cupboards accordingly ensuring that a child who only eats cornflakes is not faced with only Rice Krispies or Weetabix! For the parent who tells you that their daughter only eats bacon, eggs, mushrooms, tomatoes, fried bread and toast for breakfast a change might need to be negotiated, unless they are willing to cook this at home for their child every morning!

School/Nursery/Playgroup runs

A large part of the childminder's day is spent taxiing children to and from various schools, nurseries, groups and clubs and never has organization been so important as when timing these important journeys. I would never advise a childminder to service two or more different schools or playgroups unless the start and finishing times vary considerably and, even then, I would be very cautious. You *must* make sure that children are in school on time every day and that you are waiting for them when school finishes at the end of the day. Children should never be hanging around in the playground waiting for you because you have misjudged how long the journey will take or got caught up in traffic.

Occasionally, even with careful planning, you may be running late and it is important that you telephone the school in cases such as these, inform them of your delay and request that they keep the children indoors until your arrival. This should not be a regular occurrence as you should be altering your timing and reassessing your routine if you are unable to get to school to collect children punctually. If the playgroup, nursery and school you have decided to service are all on the same premises you shouldn't have a problem with time-keeping as it will be possible for you to ensure that all children arrive at their correct class on time. However it will need a lot of careful planning and consideration if you are intending to take children to one school for 9am whilst promising to drop another child off at a nursery somewhere else for the same time. It is obvious that one of the children is going to be late! Ideally you will only agree to service schools and nurseries in different localities if the starting times of each differ sufficiently to allow you to get both children there on time.

Likewise if you are collecting from playgroup and nursery at lunchtime, make sure that you are able to get to each on time, every time.

It has to be said that the morning school run can become boring and tedious not just for you but also for the children. If you bear in mind that you will take and collect from school twice a day, every day (not to mention the number of additional trips you may do to playgroup and nursery) it is not surprising that, after ten years or so, you may feel like you spend more time on the school premises than the headmaster does – without the benefit of his salary – and it may be necessary for you to make this time a little more enjoyable. So, rather than looking at the school run as a necessary bind try looking at it as an educational 'outing'. All the children can become involved. Plan suitable activities for the journey (this will also take the children's minds off aching legs). You could try asking the children to count how many cats they spot on the way to school or, if you are teaching the children about numbers or colours suggest that they look for house numbers with a '2' in them, or count all the red doors they see.

You will of course need to make sure that any activity you plan does not endanger the children. There is little point getting Jimmy to count the cats if he walks straight into the path of a car whilst doing so! Anything you can think of that will make the children more agreeable in the morning is worth a try, and if it means the children cooperate more readily it will certainly make your life easier.

Feeding patterns for babies

There is no denying that a hungry baby will need feeding. Whatever journeys you have to make and however busy your schedule is, feeding times should not be drastically altered. It is a good idea to work with the child's parents with regard to feeding patterns for their baby in order for things to run smoothly for you both. Obviously babies are not programmable and their feeding patterns will invariably differ from day to day and week to week but, by working in partnership with parents, you should be able to work out a suitable feeding pattern that will work for everyone. There is little point in a parent dropping her baby off with you at 8.45am ready for a 9am feed if you have four other children to get to school. The baby will either have to wait for its feed or the other children will have to be late for school and neither scenario is acceptable. Talk to the parents and let them know about your routine. If they do not have school-age children themselves they will probably never have given the school run a thought and will just assume that you are able to feed their child at the time they are used to. It is possible to please the parent, feed the baby and get the children to school on time – this simply needs a little forward planning, organization and common sense.

Toddler groups and support groups

Childminders are often able to attend toddler groups and support groups with the children in their care. Unlike playgroup and nursery, you will be expected to stay with the children at these groups as they are very much designed with the adults in mind as well as the children. Toddler groups are a great place for mothers to be able to meet up, usually once a week, and they are an excellent setting for making friends and socializing whilst the children are playing.

Alternatively, support groups are similar to toddler groups but are run by childminders for childminders and are a way for practitioners to get together to share information and experiences with one another. Childminding can often be a very lonely profession as many childminders work alone from home and the chances of meeting other adults on a daily basis other than in the school playground for five or ten minutes are limited. Support groups are usually held in village halls, churches, scout huts or schools and childminders pay a nominal fee to cover the rental charge of the building. Attending these is a great way to spend a couple of hours enjoying adult company over coffee and biscuits whilst the children play together – there *are* some perks to childminding! Many childminders look forward to their weekly meeting and these meetings can be an excellent way of keeping in touch with fellow professionals and a good way of organizing outings and fundraising events. By regularly attending support groups you will get to know other carers in your area, establish friendships, enable the children to take part in the local community and get to know what is happening in your immediate area. Support groups are also an excellent way of generating business and accessing support from fellow practitioners who understand exactly what childminding is all about.

Lunch

Depending on the number of children you are caring for and their ages, lunchtime can be almost as manic as breakfast time except you won't need to rush off to school before you have cleared away the dishes! Try to plan lunchtime to take place about half an hour after you have arrived home following the nursery or playgroup collections as this will enable the children to wind down sufficiently after their morning and give you ample time to prepare the food.

Ideally you will have planned the meal in advance and will know exactly what you are going to serve. It is not a good idea to be rushing around the kitchen like a headless chicken searching for a suitable meal whilst the children are gazing on, ravenous. Mealtimes can vary immensely from one childminding setting to another. Some childminders:

- Provide three cooked meals per day with various snacks (if you decide to do this make sure that your prices reflect the cost of the food otherwise you could find yourself seriously out of pocket if you care for several children with enormous appetites). If you provide breakfast and tea for school-aged children remember that the fee you charge must take this into account as your profit margins will suffer seriously if you don't. Remember, older children usually eat much more than younger ones and can often be ravenous after a busy day at school.

- Provide breakfast, a cooked lunch and a cold buffet tea.

- Provide breakfast, a buffet lunch and a cooked tea.

- Provide no food at all as they expect parents to provide their own.

Whatever method of food provision you decide on make sure that the parents are aware of it. If you do not provide meals it is paramount that parents understand the need for them to bring a packed lunch or ready-prepared meal to your setting. I must stress that very few childminders expect parents to provide their own food for day care children. However, many do request a packed meal for children who are collected from school each day.

Planned outings and activities

Although outings can be immensely entertaining and great fun for both the children and the childminder they also take a lot of careful planning. Ideally outings involving visits to the zoo or an adventure park that are some distance away will be planned for school holidays in order that you will not have to be back for 3–3.30pm to collect children from school. Even if you set off at 9.30am, after taking children to school, you would be rushing towards the end of the afternoon if you have to collect them again. Remember everything takes twice as long as usual when you have one young child in tow so having two or three children means that the length of time you require will be considerably increased!

If you decide to take children on planned trips or if you are intending to utilize the facilities of play gyms and swimming baths on a regular basis, consider the costs involved. A couple of pounds per child may not seem like a lot of money but, if you are taking three children and provide them all with a snack or a drink at the end of the session, together with the admission charge for yourself you could well be spending £15 per week on one activity. This amount will be increased if you need to pay for petrol or bus fares to travel to the venue. £15–£20 per week for one activity is expensive and if you are intending to pay for everything from your own income you will quickly see your wages begin to dwindle. If you are intending to entertain children in this way you would be advised to ask parents for their opinion (it is necessary for you to obtain written permission from parents anyway before transporting children in a car or taking them on outings) and see whether they are prepared to fund all or some of the cost of the outings. Some parents, happy that their children are taking part in extra swimming lessons or enjoying exercise in a play gym, will be only too happy to stump up the extra costs every week – others will not. You should think carefully about this dilemma as it is unfair to take money from two parents and fund the third yourself. You may be able to come to some arrangement with all the parents; perhaps you could limit the visit to once a fortnight or request only a percentage of the entrance fee and take your own drinks and snacks. Never assume that a parent's refusal to pay is down to them being mean or miserly – often finances are tight and many working parents have to budget sensibly – fun trips to the play gym will not be on their list of priorities if their child needs a new pair of shoes!

School collections

As mentioned earlier, taking and collecting children from school should be planned with military precision to avoid you turning up late. Children should never be left unattended in the playground because you have failed to turn up on time. You should be the one standing in the playground not the child! Always give yourself ample time for the journey to school. After you have done the trip several times you will soon recognize which routes to avoid and be able to time the journey well. The roads will probably be quieter in an afternoon when you collect the children than they were in the morning when you dropped them off as you will not have the heavy commuter traffic of people rushing to work to contend with. If you are collecting children later, say 5pm because they have attended an after school club, then bear in mind that traffic at this time may well be heavy once again with businesses finishing for the day.

Tea

Provided you are certain in your mind about exactly what you plan to serve at teatime there is no need for this meal to be any more difficult than lunchtime even with the added number of school children joining the day care ones. If you allow the older children to dictate what they want to eat, however, then you are asking for trouble! Ideally you should know the preferences of each child present and aim to provide a meal that will be acceptable to everyone. However, if a child decides to be 'difficult' and requests a sandwich rather than the cooked meal you usually provide, think carefully before giving in. There may of course be a perfectly valid reason for his request – the child may be feeling a little under the weather and the appetite is affected, or the child may simply not be very hungry due to having had a larger than usual lunch. To avoid changing your own plans you could suggest that he eats the same as everyone else albeit a smaller portion. Handling the situation in this manner acknowledges the child's request whilst also avoiding the possibility of future problems if other children start to request different meals. Obviously if a child is completely uninterested in a meal you are not at liberty to force-feed them and their parents should be informed of their refusal to eat when the child is collected.

Try to make mealtimes as enjoyable as possible. They should be sociable occasions that everyone is involved in. Children eat much better when they sit down to a meal with others and often even 'faddy' eaters can be encouraged to eat a reasonable amount of food when sitting at the table and enjoying a meal together.

You may be requested to cater for special diets and many childminders are a little apprehensive as to what this actually entails and become worried that they may give the child something to eat which is unsuitable. Although these fears are perfectly reasonable catering for special diets need not be a problem provided you understand exactly what the child can and cannot eat. Obviously if the child has an allergy to certain food stuffs then failure to cater for them correctly could result in them becoming ill. However, by talking to the parent and ensuring that you know exactly what the child is able to eat you can eliminate any potential dangers.

Vegetarian diets and diets based around religious beliefs are just as important as diets catering for allergies. It is *not* of course acceptable to pass a pork sausage off as a vegetarian one simply because this is all you have in the freezer, and if you agree to cater for certain diets you must make sure you carry your promise through.

Whether a parent requests a 'special' diet or not it is paramount that the meals and snacks you do provide are healthy and nutritional. Always bear in mind that the quality of a child's diet is crucial at all ages. You may be aware that the child is fed junk food at home but this is no excuse for you to do the same whilst they are in your care. Some children are faddy eaters who refuse to eat vegetables or try new foods and you will need to show patience and understanding in these cases. Often a particular food can be refused one day and eagerly eaten the next! Never assume that just because a child doesn't like bananas at two years old they will still not like them at three years old. Keep re-introducing foods regularly as a child's tastes develop and change continually. You can help children to eat a healthy diet by:

- Offering a variety of foods. This doesn't mean feeding a hot spicy curry to a two-year-old – use your common sense and offer foods suitable to the child's age.

- Offering a healthy amount of food. Too much food will result in a child becoming overweight and too little will result in malnutrition. The correct amount of food will depend on the age and size of the child.

- Offering food which is rich in starch and fibre.

- Offering lots of fruit and vegetables.

- Avoiding offering fatty or sugary food.

- Avoiding offering drinks which contain a lot of sugar – stick to water or fruit juice.

- Encouraging children to enjoy mealtimes and to see these as sociable events.

Homework

Homework can often cause problems for childminders. Parents want their children to do it at your house, children don't want to do it at anyone's house! Should childminders be expected to force children into doing their homework? This is a common problem faced by many childminders on a daily basis and the simple truth is childminders should provide a suitable quiet area for children to do their homework and be available to offer support if required but it is not the responsibility of the childminder to ensure that children have completed their homework. It is important that parents are made to understand how busy teatime is for childminders and that valuable time cannot be spent bribing, coaxing or begging children to do their homework. Completing homework on time is a matter of 'parental' responsibility.

Not all parents expect you to help their child with their homework and indeed some prefer their children to participate in games and activities whilst in the childminding setting leaving homework for when they get home. This is all a matter of preference and should of course be discussed with the child's parents. It may be that parents don't get much time during the week to help their child with their homework, spelling tests and reading and they will appreciate your assistance. It is a good idea to get the parents to discuss what is expected in terms of homework with their child so that they understand that it is their parent who is requesting that they carry out their homework at your house and not you. Doing this eliminates the problem of the child thinking that it is you who is insisting that they do their maths, geography etc.

It is all well and good helping a six-year-old with their spellings and reading but how would you manage if a 12-year-old asked you to help them with algebra? If you are not confident in any areas of a child's homework – be honest! It is far better to say that you have forgotten what you learned when you were at school (even if you never understood it in the first place) than to blindly work your way through making a complete hash of it and confusing the child. Rest assured when the child comes bottom in the class in algebra everyone in the school will know it was you who helped them with their homework!

Home time

The end of the day is by far the most problematic. This is not just because the children and you are tired after a long day but because there are usually parents present. There is nothing like a parent to upset the smooth running of things! Children will invariably play up when a parent walks through the door regardless of whether they are their parent or not. They play up at this time quite simply because they think they can. It is quite normal for a child to believe that no one will reprimand them if there is another adult present. Quite where they get this idea from is anyone's guess, however they will continue to play up if they get away with it, so the simple answer to this scenario is don't let them! Never turn a blind eye to behaviour that you would not normally allow. Remember that it is still your home and your rules apply whether there is one or a 101 adults in the room.

Children can sometimes feel a little confused when their own parents come to collect them and are often undecided as to who is 'boss'. They will often test this kind of situation by playing up.

You can almost see the child daring you to tell them off in front of their parents and, if you have a good relationship with the parents, and have explained your policies thoroughly, this should not be a problem as both you and the parent should reprimand an unruly child – the shock alone when two adults reprimand them should be enough to quieten the child down!

You may find yourself in the awkward situation of having a child who doesn't want to go home. In my experience this can be for a number of reasons although rarely is it because they are unhappy with their parents or home life (although obviously this is something which should be considered in extreme cases). The more common reasons for a child refusing to cooperate are:

- They are having a good time with their friends.

- They are engrossed in a game or with a particular toy.

- They are looking for a reaction from their parents.

- They are looking for a reaction from you.

The easiest way to avoid these scenarios is:

1   To make sure that children are ready for their parent's arrival. This is obviously easier to do if parents collect their children at the same time every day. Make sure that the child has finished their game and helped to tidy away. Reading a short story is a good way of winding down in time for parents to arrive.

2   Not to let the child see that their behaviour is winding you up. If the child thinks that their delay tactics are bothering you they will carry them on. Ignore any unwanted behaviour and carry on with the task of tidying up to let the child see that being uncooperative is not working.

3   (In very extreme cases) to have the child's shoes and coat

on so that the parent can literally take them from you at the door.

Some parents in my setting have been known to pretend to go without their child hoping that this will hurry them along and get them to cooperate – be prepared for the opposite and think how you will handle the situation if the child happily waves at the window whilst their mother hurries up the garden path!

8

Additional requests

You might think that a childminder's job is difficult enough without parents adding additional requests. Settling crying children into the setting, dealing with challenging behaviour, coaxing children to eat a healthy breakfast, and preventing World War Three from erupting in your living room over who is going to be the first to play with Thomas the Tank Engine would exhaust most people but when all this happens before 9am it can be rather taxing!

When experiencing this kind of morning you will invariably get the odd parent who will drop off their child saying something along the lines of 'I hate to ask you this, and you can say no if it's not convenient but could you take Jemima to her ballet class/hair appointment/doctor's appointment at 4pm this afternoon?' – 'Thanks, you're a saint!' they add, before turning and rushing off in case the full implications of their request dawn on you before they have left and you tell them that it won't be possible for you to carry out their request without huge disruption to your routine, and inconvenience to the other children. After the parent has gone you are left with the dilemma of how to juggle school-aged children, a baby and two toddlers in order for you to carry out this additional parental request at what is probably one of the most inconvenient times of the day – teatime!

So how exactly can childminders deal with these additional requests successfully without causing chaos and mayhem? Of course you are not obliged to take children to the doctor's or hairdresser's and you would be quite within your rights to refuse such a request if it makes life difficult for you or inconveniences others. However if it is possible and you genuinely don't mind being put out a little it is sometimes in your own interests to go along with things for a quiet life. Remember though, if it hasn't inconvenienced you the first time, or if it has and you don't say anything, you may well be expected to do it on a regular basis! If an additional request proves awkward but you agree to alter your routine to accommodate the parent's wishes, never make the child feel as if they are causing you a huge headache. Sighing and moaning as you strap them into the car and slam the door shut will make them feel awkward and guilty when, after all, they probably prefer to stay at your house than see the doctor anyway!

If you do agree to help out a parent in this way and it has caused you a lot of inconvenience point it out to the parent politely and make sure that they understand that you have accommodated them this time as a 'one-off' but that you are unable to do it on anything other than one-off occasions, and with prior arrangement.

If you do agree to chauffeur children to clubs and classes make sure that the timing does not cause you too much inconvenience. If you don't want to accommodate a parent's request or you simply can't do as they ask then say so!

Doctor's and health visitor's appointments

Ideally these appointments should be carried out by the child's parents. You, the childminder, do not have any rights with regard to a child's health care and if the child has a doctor's appointment usually due to a health problem and they are prescribed medication, often to begin immediately, you will be unable to administer it without prior written consent from the parent. Another point for consideration is of course if the child needs to see a doctor for a health issue it may be that the doctor diagnoses a problem which may effectively mean that the child should not be in childcare. For example, a rash may turn out to be contagious, a weeping eye may actually be conjunctivitis and, in cases such as these, the child should not be mixing with other children and they will need to be collected immediately leaving you not only with a child who is not well, but also with the dilemma of contacting their parent and insisting that they collect their child immediately.

Obviously if you only care for one child during the week or if you have a day when you are quieter than others, then you may be able to incorporate doctor's or health visitor's appointments and, should the child have a contagious illness, you may even agree to continue to carry on caring for them provided of course that you are not caring for any other children at the time (there is a possibility of course that you or other members of your family may catch the illness and this is something which you should always bear in mind in cases such as these).

Routine health visitor appointments are often carried out by childminders, as these are usually just progress checks to record the child's height and weight and they rarely result in any problems which may cause concern. However you may like to think about how you would deal with things if the health visitor spots a particular problem with the child's development. For example, a minor hearing disability (this often occurs when the child has or is just getting over a cold which may cause a temporary loss or impairment of the child's hearing). How would you cope, however, if this 'minor' impairment turned out to be a more serious problem? Would you be able to inform the parents of the health visitor's findings in a sensitive manner and without causing undue concern? You will need to convey exactly what the health visitor has told you, without elaborating or omitting details depending on how the parents react to the news, and ensure that they are aware of any necessary follow-up treatment or appointments. It is not appropriate to telephone the parents hysterically the moment you get home and say that the health visitor says 'little Martyn is as deaf as a post!' Decorum and sensitivity are needed in cases such as these and you will need to offer support if and when it is needed.

If you are not confident dealing with any health issues in this way then you must inform the parent and tell them you would feel happier if they took their child to the doctor or health visitor themselves. Remember you are not obliged to agree to any such additional requests and are quite within your rights to refuse to do so.

Hairdresser's appointments

It has to be said that, unlike doctor and health visitor appointments, which are often only made between 9am and 6pm Monday to Friday, hair appointments are much more flexible and the need for inconveniencing an already busy childminder should not really arise. However you would be surprised how many times parents are unable to take their child to have their hair cut, and when little Robert resorts to putting his hair in pig tails just so that he can see where he is going, you may feel you have to give in and agree to take him to the hairdresser's! Always bear in mind how many children you will be caring for, and if a parent asks you to take their child for a haircut and makes an afternoon appointment when you have five other children to care for you should politely explain why this is not possible. Not only should you recognize the inconvenience this may put on the hairdresser – six unruly children running around a busy salon is not ideal – but you should also take into account the opinions of other parents whose children you are caring for. By pleasing one parent and attending a hairdressing appointment you may well risk upsetting the parents of the other five children. How would you feel if you were paying someone to care for your child and instead of giving them their tea they were dragging them around hair salons? Professionalism is paramount and conducting your business in this way is not professional.

Again if you only have one child to consider, and you don't mind taking them to the hairdresser's, then this will not be a problem. If you have other people to consider then you should politely explain the situation to the child's parent and suggest that they make an appointment at a mutually convenient time in future or, if you really do not wish to take the child to the hairdresser's, then inform the parent and suggest they make a weekend appointment if they are unable to get to a salon after work.

After school clubs

Many schools run clubs after the usual school hours and you may find yourself in the position of caring for a child, or several children, who would like to attend one or more of these clubs during the week. This should rarely pose a problem if you only have one child to collect of if all the children you usually collect decide to attend the club in question. However, if you usually collect several children and only one child wishes to go to the club you may find yourself having to travel backwards and forwards. These types of school clubs usually last between an hour and an hour and a half and, if you have a substantial distance to travel to and from school, agreeing to pick up from after school clubs may be an unwelcome request you could well do without. You will need to consider the other children in your care before agreeing to collect from any clubs and take into account the time you serve tea and the times when parents are likely to be collecting children from you. You will not be popular if you are at school collecting a child from drama club if there are two other parents standing on your doorstep in the pouring rain waiting to collect their children. Think about the bad weather and traffic and what problems these are likely to pose on your journey. You should also consider the care of any younger children who will be ferried backwards and forwards in this way and may well be spending hours on end strapped in a car whilst you collect children from their various clubs and classes.

Another major consideration when agreeing to collect children from clubs is one of finances. Will you charge parents for the hour or so that their child spends at a club? Bear in mind that:

- It is highly unlikely that you will be able to fill this place.

- You will probably be expected to keep the place open for the child in the event that the club is cancelled for any reason.

- You will incur extra petrol expenses if you are making additional journeys.

Rest assured you will get parents who are not happy paying you if their child is not in attendance, even after you have explained your reasons, and this will be doubly so if the club also charges a fee.

When additional requests encroach on the service you provide or threaten to jeopardize own family commitments

Obviously if a parent asks you to take their child to a class or an appointment and it is easy for you to carry out this request without adding too much disruption to your usual daily routine then it would be better to do so rather than appear awkward or uncompromising. However there may be times when a parent makes a request which will prove difficult or even impossible for you to carry out and in these cases it is paramount that you say something. As mentioned, it is not acceptable to inconvenience other children in order to keep one family happy nor should you be expected to go above and beyond what could be classed as reasonably acceptable requests in order to appease paying customers. You are a trained professional with a business to run. It is important that childminders make it clear to parents that although they are willing to help out as much as possible, there may be times when it is neither possible nor practical for them to carry out certain requests.

If you have a parent who regularly asks you to take or collect their child from various clubs and appointments which proves difficult you will need to speak to them and explain how difficult it is for you to do these things. Often occasional requests can be catered for but when they become regular routines you may find yourself faced with problems you had not anticipated. Point out to the parent that the contract you have with them does not stipulate these additional requests and that they are posing problems for you. If a parent asks to alter their contract to take into account collection from clubs or classes make sure that you think things through carefully. If this is causing you problems now it won't make things any easier by adding it to the contract. In fact it will make it more difficult as what was initially a polite request will now become an extra demand! You should also think about how you would deal with the situation if you were faced with the dilemma of collecting different children from different clubs and classes several nights per week. How do you decide which child you can accommodate and which you cannot? Are you going to run yourself ragged trying to be in three or four places at once or end up pleasing no one leaving you with unhappy children feeling as if they are missing out? You might like to ask the children which clubs they prefer and go with the majority, but this can of course also cause problems particularly if the parents become involved in the debate.

Let us now look at situations which, although they may not encroach on your other childminding duties, may well inconvenience you and your own family commitments. What if your own child has football practice or a piano lesson and due to a parent collecting their child late on a regular basis, your child is missing out? Many childminders think that being inconvenienced in this way is par for the course and is a downside of the job. This is not a fair assumption and you should not be expected to work late regularly in this way Obviously financial issues may be at stake here and you do not wish to upset the parent by saying something about their bad time-keeping in case it results in them taking their custom elsewhere. However have you considered that the parent may not even realize that they are inconveniencing you in this way, and if you said something the situation may be simply rectified? Parents sometimes go home or shopping after they have finished work, and if when they collect their child they are happy and having fun and you do not appear put out in any way they will not see the necessity for good time-keeping. One of the downsides of working from home is that customers often fail to understand that you are 'working' whenever there is a child on your premises and that you prefer to finish on time just like them!

All in all additional requests only pose a problem if you allow them to. If you are not happy carrying out such duties then you must say so, explaining your reasons. However, if the requests do not inconvenience you then avoid making a mountain out of a molehill. Pleasing the child and the parent when possible will ultimately win you 'Brownie points' and reiterate just how valuable your service is!

9
Problems

Problems can, and will, occur from time to time. Even the most patient, helpful and organized childminder, who seems to take everything in their stride and who thinks that nothing is too much trouble, will at times come across an irate parent, an unhappy child, or both! No one is perfect and there will be times when someone disagrees with you, stretches the boundaries to breaking point or tests your patience just a little too far! Avoid the temptation to snap and refrain from telling them exactly what you think of their behaviour and unreasonable demands and always remember to act like the professional that you are. Even if the parent rants and raves until they go red in the face never (and I repeat never) shout back. Remain composed and dignified when dealing with problems – it is possible to get your point of view across in a much more productive manner when you don't shout and lose your temper and you will have the smug satisfaction when things do calm down of not having resorted to acting like a banshee!

Always listen to a parent, or indeed a child, if they are drawing your attention to a particular problem, and never interrupt or defend yourself whilst they are speaking as this usually adds fuel to the fire and irritates the already irate person even more. Make notes mentally of the things you do not agree with and, when they have put their message across, this is the time to let them know your opinion on the matter.

It may be that the particular issue in question is something that you are already aware of and indeed you may also have an opinion on and, if this is the case, then let the parent know your point of view. If, however, the parent is bringing a particular issue to your attention that you were not aware of it may be that you need time to consider what is being said to you, act upon it and get back to them with your findings. Again if this is the case, explain your intentions to the parent and see things through. Never promise to investigate a problem or issue just to appease a parent and then conveniently forget as soon as they walk out of the room. They will not forget and if, at a later date, the issue is raised again and you have done nothing to sort it out you stand to look either foolish or unconcerned, neither of which is good for business.

Always remember that an issue which seems relatively small and inconsequential to you could well be something which is affecting the parent or their child considerably and all matters should be dealt with appropriately and promptly.

Top tips for dealing with problems:

- Listen to exactly what is being said.
- Make mental notes of the points you wish to raise.
- Never interrupt when you are being told something.
- Never shout or become angry – even if the parent does.
- When putting your own point of view across, be polite, courteous and clear.
- Think before you speak.
- Speak calmly but firmly.
- Be open to suggestions and be prepared to compromise.

The best and most successful way of dealing with problems or issues is to tackle them head on, openly and honestly. Talking to the people involved, listening and compromising are all ways of solving problems without the need for disagreements or heated arguments. Rarely, if ever, does an argument solve a problem. Negotiation and seeing things from all perspectives are usually what is needed in order to successfully sort out a problem. Although it is often difficult to predict when problems may arise there are certain areas which attract more conflict than others and these are the areas which will require most of your attention.

Contract disputes

Contracts should be watertight with no room for misunderstanding or misinterpretation. You should make sure that *every* area of your childminding service is covered and that all agreements made with parents are outlined in the contract. You may feel strange presenting each parent with a 40-page 'book' as a contract but believe me you will be grateful when the parent raises an issue regarding fees and you can refer her to page 26 paragraph 4 (c) – problem solved! Seriously though, it is important that you include all the vital, relevant information.

Contracts should clearly state the days and hours you care for the child and the fees charged. It is absolutely essential that you ensure that parents are aware of what is expected of them in the case of paying fees for holidays, illness, occasional days off etc. and whether you expect full fee or a retainer. You may know exactly what the parent should pay but never *assume* that something you have agreed in conversation during the initial interview will be remembered by the parent several months down the line. *Always* put vital information and important facts in writing and get the parent to sign in agreement. Some parents will adhere to the contract diligently sticking to their side of the bargain as if their lives depended on it. Others will see the contract as insignificant, and although they are *aware* of the content of the contract they will still raise issues and try to renegotiate things in their favour at every opportunity. If your contract is watertight and includes all the necessary relevant points you shouldn't have any problems enforcing it. Remember that you do not have to write your own contracts; the National Childminding Association (NCMA) sells pre-written contracts for childminders at specially reduced rates and, if you are at all unsure of what to include in a contract, do consider purchasing them from the NCMA.

The actual drawing up of a contract is a process of negotiation between you and the child's parent. Contracts should be filled in *together*. There is little point in completing a contract yourself in the vain hope that parents will agree to everything you demand – this is not negotiation! If you cannot agree the terms of a contract with a parent so that the content suits both parties then it may not be possible for you to care for the child. You may, for example, expect parents to pay for your service 47 weeks per annum (the other five weeks being your holiday); however if you care for the child of a teacher who has 13 weeks' holiday per annum they may not be happy paying you for the remaining eight weeks, particularly if they will never use your service during that time. This is an issue which will need to be negotiated and a compromise will need to be found if you are to successfully care for the child. You may like to consider agreeing to charge half the usual fee during these eight weeks in order to make the cost more acceptable to the parent, however you must ensure that you can afford to take this loss in earnings before agreeing to care for the child. If five weeks at no fee and eight at half result in financial difficulties for you then you should not agree to the reduction, as resentment will soon set in.

Once a contract is signed by all parties it becomes legally binding. It is therefore essential that you do not commit yourself to something you cannot carry through, as not only will this put you in breach of contract, it will also mean that parents can make a claim in the small claims court if they can prove the contract has been broken. Likewise the same applies to the parent, therefore both parties must completely understand what is expected of them before signing.

Fees

Probably the most common issue for problems with regard to childminding, fees can cause real headaches if not handled correctly! There are a few very important rules that you should abide by when it comes to negotiating fees and these are:

1   Always negotiate for childminding fees to be paid in advance.

2   Never let fees go unpaid – even if you are good friends with the parent in question. You have provided a service and you can expect to be paid for that service.

3   Make sure that parents understand what retainer fees are for and when they will be expected to pay them.

4   Review fees regularly. It is more acceptable to parents if you increase your fees by a small amount every year than to wait two or three years and increase them by a large amount.

5   If a parent regularly pays late, consider introducing a late payment fee until the debt is cleared. This should encourage parents to pay on time.

6   If you are having difficulty getting a parent to pay their fees, ask them if they are having any financial problems (in a sensitive way!) and try to negotiate a payment method that is acceptable to you both. It could be that the parent's own pay day has been altered making it difficult for them

to pay you on the originally agreed day and renegotiating your payment day with them may be all that is required.

7   If, even after negotiation, payment is not forthcoming it may be necessary for you to withdraw your service until the outstanding debt has been paid. Allowing a parent to add to their existing debt week after week will be of no benefit to anyone and you risk working a considerable number of weeks without payment. If you feel certain you are not going to be paid it is better to withdraw your services after a couple of weeks and lose this amount than to continue caring for the child, perhaps for several months clocking up expenses such as food and drink, and still see no money for your efforts at the end of it all.

> **REMEMBER:** The bigger the debt – the harder it is to recoup. Never allow childminding fees to go unpaid.

Despite the fact that contracts are legally binding, this will not give you a complete guarantee that you will be paid on time. Some parents will break their contracts without a second thought and it will then be up to you to decide whether the matter is worth taking to the small claims court or whether you should write it off and put it down to experience. Being a good judge of character and ensuring that parents completely understand your contract and what is expected of them will go a long way to ensuring that contract disputes do not occur.

Holidays

It has to be said that when a childminder books a holiday it can cause a great deal of headache for their customers. However, unless you are prepared to work 52 weeks of the year resigning yourself to never having another holiday during the duration of

your childminding career then this is something that you will have
to deal with. As with many areas of running your own business
the key to taking time off without causing too much disruption is
to *plan ahead*. Always give your customers plenty of notice of your
intended holiday in order for them to have the time either to
arrange to take their own annual leave at the same time as yours or
to arrange childcare cover for the weeks you are unavailable.
Everyone needs a holiday from time to time in order to relax,
recharge their batteries and take stock of things; however it is
perfectly understandable for parents to become irate if you inform
them on a Friday that you are jetting off for six weeks to the
Caribbean sunshine the following day!

As a childminder you will probably have a number of people
reliant on your service. If you fail to give sufficient notice of your
intention to go on holiday not only do you risk the wrath of your
customers, some of whom will look elsewhere for childcare
permanently in order to avoid the same thing happening again,
you will also be doing yourself and your business a lot of harm.
Word will get around that you are unreliable and that you put
your own needs well ahead of your customers – this is not a good
impression to portray and it is certainly very unprofessional.

If possible, it is a good idea to give your customers some
indication of how many weeks per annum you intend to take for
holidays and an approximate time of the year you expect these to
happen. At the beginning of every year try to plan your holidays.
You do not have to book them immediately but if you are
intending to take five weeks' holiday during the whole of the year
inform your customers and explain that although no dates have
been booked yet, you anticipate taking perhaps two weeks at
Easter, two in the summer and your final week at Christmas.
Exact dates can be confirmed at a later date when you have
booked your holiday. However, by giving the parents as much
notice as possible in advance you will make the job of finding
alternative childcare whilst you are away so much easier.

I would recommend that you give parents *at least* four weeks'
notice of your intended holiday dates, longer if possible, in order
for them to decide what to do. You may get parents who expect
you to book your own holidays around them, but although this
may seem a good solution to the parents, it is not so easy for you if
you care for children from several families. It is far better for you
to tell the parents when you are going on holiday and for them to
work around your dates than for you and all your other customers
to work around one particular family – even from a fairness point
of view this is not practical. Provided you give parents as much
notice as possible of your intention to go on holiday you should
find them amicable.

Another point you will need to make sure parents are in
agreement with is any fees which are payable during these holiday
periods. As self-employed people, childminders are not legally
entitled to holiday pay. However many do charge for time off as
they are of the opinion that if their customers get paid holidays
then they should be willing to pay for their childminder's holiday.
Not all parents see things this way, particularly if they are having
to pay someone else to care for their children whilst you are away
and it is important that you negotiate with the parents what, if
any, fee they are expected to pay whilst you are on holiday. Some
childminders will charge full fee whilst they are on holiday, some
will charge half as they will not have any overheads if they are not
working, whilst others waive the fee believing that it is not really
appropriate to charge for a service that is not available.
Whatever you decide to charge is entirely up to you but make sure
that parents understand your fees and how much they will be
expected to pay. Charging full fee for holidays may sound great to
you but if other childminders in your area waive their fees during
holiday periods you may find your valued customers looking
elsewhere for more reasonable rates. Never be greedy – charge a
reasonable rate for a good service rather than an extortionate rate
for a mediocre service and you stand to generate, and keep,
business!

Illness

What happens when the childminder is ill? Does everything fall apart? Are the children left to fend for themselves? Do they go hungry? Of course not! No one is indispensable – you included – although it has to be said that when the childminder falls ill it causes a huge amount of disruption!

Everyone gets ill from time to time and succumbing to illness is unavoidable. How much time you take off due to illness and how frequently you fall ill will have an impact on your business. If you are, by nature, a person who falls ill easily or has a medical problem that surfaces periodically you should think carefully about whether a career caring for children is for you. As a childminder, without backup cover, you risk letting a lot of people down if you are constantly taking time off work to nurse a bad back or take to your bed with a nasty migraine. Although you may well be unable to avoid these occurrences parents' understanding of your medical problems will wear thin if you let them down on a regular basis. However falling ill to flu is something that everyone is prone to from time to time and of course there is no way you can give parents notice of your intention to take time off to be ill! It is in the main the responsibility of the parents to ensure that they have backup childcare cover for situations such as these, but if you know of a childminder who is willing to provide short-term cover, and who has the available places to accommodate your customers when you are ill, it is always a good idea to be in a position to suggest alternative cover for parents at short notice.

Many childminders feel guilty if they need to take time off work and indeed, unless it is absolutely necessary, many trundle through the days as best they can refusing to give in to their illness or take time off. Money is once again a major bone of contention for self-employed people who take time off through illness. Most employed people are entitled to some form of sick pay whereas childminders usually take a cut in pay if they need a couple of days off to recuperate. Although some childminders will charge full fee even if they are unable to work due to illness, arguing that the majority of bad colds and sick bugs are a result of the job, many others waive their fees if they need time off for illness – this of course often means that the childminder returns to work before having fully recovered in order to start earning a living again and may then continue struggling through ill health.

The other scenario childminders are faced with is when the children are ill. How ill should a child be before being turned away from the setting? Contagious illnesses such as chicken pox and conjunctivitis can be seen and so are easy to diagnose. However, what happens if a child has a very bad tummy ache or ear ache and is obviously in a lot of pain but poses no threat to the other children present? Coughs and colds are very common and though no one would expect a parent to take time off work every time their child sneezes, when would the child be deemed unfit to be in a childminding setting? Should a child be at home with a temperature? Many of these questions can be successfully answered if you know the child well and are aware of how they usually react to certain situations. Experience is a great tool and you will be able to make an educated guess with regard to the signs and symptoms of illness once you have witnessed them a couple of times.

How you deal with parents who refuse to acknowledge when their child is ill and should not be in the setting is a whole new ball game. Some will accept the inevitable and make alternative arrangements, albeit reluctantly, but others will deny everything. Even if a child has chicken pox covering 90 per cent of their body you will get the odd parent who categorically insists that their child has a simple allergic reaction to something and they may even insist that their GP has told them this! How do you respond to this kind of scenario? Stick to your guns! Tell the parent you have seen enough chicken pox to know one when it is staring you in the face and explain that you are unable to care for their child.

It is a brave childminder who will do this but, unfortunately, such drastic action is sometimes necessary. The parent will then either respect your authority and professionalism – without admitting they were wrong – or pack up their child and belongings and find alternative childcare – permanently!

The simple truth of the matter is that a child who is suffering from a contagious illness of any kind should not be in a childminding setting mixing with others. A child suffering from a minor cough or cold, provided they are well 'in themselves' and happy to play and take part in the activities on offer should be allowed into the setting and monitored regularly. Any child running a high temperature or who is obviously in a lot of pain should not be in a childminding setting. Once again you need to think carefully about the fees you will charge for a child who is not in the setting due to illness. Charging half the usual fee or waiving the fee altogether may see you left short on pay day particularly if the child succumbs to a lot of illnesses. Charging full may see parents bringing their children even if they are unwell in the hope that you 'will not notice' how unwell their child is!

Potty training

Potty training is never an easy issue to deal with. How quickly the child grasps the thread and how helpful the parent is when working with you will determine just how easy or difficult this task is going to be. I have cared for children who, at two years old, have taken just a couple of weeks to become completely 'dry' and who have never had an accident or 'forgotten' to use the toilet. There have also been others who at four years old frequently soil themselves and seem not to care one iota! Children are all very different and, when it comes to potty training, much will depend on the parents' attitudes as much as the children themselves. Some parents are so determined to get their child out of nappies that they go the whole hog, buying training pants with pretty patterns on, reward charts, stickers and bags of sweets and toys by the bucketful to bribe their children with. When at the end of the first month the child is stuffed until they are sick on sweets, the parents need a bank loan to pay their bill at Hamley's and the child is still leaving wet patches all over the carpet, they are at their wits' end! Put it this way – if you were constantly being offered tasty treats and indulged with presents would you want it all to come to an abrupt end? Of course not, so little wonder children who experience this kind of treatment may well still be 'potty training' well into their teens!

Potty training must be kept in perspective. I do not know of any child who has started school still wearing a nappy (unless they have a medical problem) therefore it is highly likely that little Harold who is still experiencing the odd accident at three years old will be completely toilet trained by the time he hits reception class, therefore is it really necessary for his mother to get so stressed out every time he has a drink or jiggles up and down? By easing up on the pressure parents can in fact help their children to train more quickly. Let's face it, it is not the 'be all and end all' to have your child out of nappies by the time they begin to walk, is it?

There are of course advantages to getting children out of nappies, not least because of the costs involved. Disposable nappies, in addition to being bad for the environment, also cost a fortune. However, if you think this is a good reason not to buy disposable nappies think how you would feel as a childminder if faced with an earth mother and her newborn tightly wrapped in a fluffy white terry nappy! Nappy buckets, sterilizing liquid, soggy cloth nappies and a mountain of washing – pass the Pampers immediately!!!

Manners

Parents are the first educators of their children but what do you do if you are faced with a child who has never learned the art of basic manners? It is of course not really the child's fault if at eight years old they have never been taught to say 'please' and 'thank you' but it can be seen as ever so slightly rude when a child snatches something from you without so much as an upward glance. You can go a long way to counteracting this kind of issue by writing and implementing a behaviour policy that incorporates manners. Explain to the children, and their parents, that you expect basic manners and courtesy from those present in your setting. You can encourage children to use manners by displaying the same politeness towards them and by explaining that you expect basic manners to be used. It may of course take some time before a child fully understands what is expected of them, particularly if they resort to not using manners elsewhere, and you should show patience and understanding in these cases.

Although it should not really be the childminder's job to *teach* basic manners to a child, particularly one who is much older and at school, it can sometimes be a necessity if you are to feel at all valued and respected, particularly if the child spends a good deal of their time in your care.

Sleep patterns

How do you keep a tired child awake? This really is the million dollar question and if only I had a pound for every time I have been asked to do this I would be a very rich woman indeed!

Try telling a parent that it is impossible to keep their child awake from 7.30am until 6pm and your protestations will surely fall on deaf ears. Explain that you consider prodding a sleepy child to keep them awake cruel and they will defend themselves to the death! There is one thing for certain: you cannot keep a tired child awake any more than you can make an 'untired' child go to sleep, and anyone who has ever tried this will know exactly what I am talking about! Hypnosis may work, so might trying to bore the child to death, but neither is recommended. There are of course a number of reasons why parents may not wish their children to have a sleep during the day, none of which will be of any consolation to you when you have tried unsuccessfully for the past hour to coax the child to eat their tea when they can barely sit up and keep their eyes open. To avoid the issue of sleep disagreements the simplest way is to tell the parent that you will take your cue from the child. If the child appears sleepy (head slumped forward in the rice pudding is often a good way of knowing, as is a loud snore coming from the dressing-up corner), then put them to bed. Often only half an hour is all that is needed to revive the child and help them to cope with the rest of the day. Of course some children, once asleep, will be oblivious to what is going on around them for the next few hours and even dropping a bomb on them would fail to make them stir – a childminder's dream? – and they may well then be wide awake for the next ten hours making bed time a nightmare (literally) for the parents. This is when you will be told under no circumstances must little Jimmy be allowed to sleep during the day. Understandable but still impossible! Talk to the parents and work out a sleep pattern which is acceptable not just to Jimmy and his parents but also to you.

You can see from this chapter that problems when childminding come in all shapes and sizes and what is completely acceptable to one family would not be tolerated by another in a million years! The most important thing for everyone to remember, parents included, is that when you are providing a service for a number of children and their families there is a fine balancing act involved in the smooth running of everyday tasks. Upset the apple cart and you could be collecting bruised fruit for many weeks! Parents need to feel that their preferences and wishes have been taken into account but it is essential that you too lay down some basic rules that everyone is expected to abide by in order to ensure that you can carry out your duties to the best of your ability and to suit everyone, rather than end up meeting yourself coming backwards just to please one parent or child whilst completely ignoring the rest. It is all too easy to listen to the parent who 'shouts the loudest', 'demands the most' or is simply 'intimidating' but this is both unacceptable and unnecessary. A parent who sees your predicament and sympathizes with you should not have their own feelings overshadowed by another who sees nothing but themselves. If you feel a parent is demanding too much from you in terms of time and effort and the rest of the children are suffering as a consequence then you must say something. If you have four children to care for after school for two hours and spend one of those hours helping one child with their homework, what chance do the other three have? It is your job to find a way to help all the children and give each one their share of your individual attention, and if this is not acceptable to one particular parent, then it may be better if they find a childminder who has just one or at most just two children to care for.

Working with another childminder or assistant

Although the majority of childminders work alone some choose either to work with a fellow childminder or employ an assistant. Working with someone can have many advantages such as:

- Being able to share ideas.
- Enjoying the company of another adult.
- Being able to offer reassurance to one another.
- Offering more flexibility.

- Having a backup practitioner around in the event of an emergency or illness (always make sure that numbers are not exceeded).

- Costs can be shared.

- The adult:child ratio may be increased making earning potential higher.

There are however problems which may occur when employing an assistant or working with a fellow childminding practitioner and these should be looked at closely before taking on such an enormous commitment.

If you employ an assistant you will be responsible for:

- Interviewing and making the correct decision with regard to whom to employ.

- Paying wages including Tax and National Insurance Contributions.

- The smooth running of the business, including being confident in setting tasks and giving instructions.

- Solving any issues which may arise between your employee and your customers – you will remain the boss and as such any problems or disagreements will have to be sorted by you!

If you decide to work with another childminder you may also come across several more problems such as:

- Deciding whose house to use as the business premises.

- Working out wages and expenses. It is obvious that more expenses will be incurred by the person whose home is being used as the childminding setting and this can cause resentment and disagreement if things are not worked out fairly.

- Differences in work attitude.

10
Writing and implementing policies

Perhaps one of the most difficult areas of childminding is recognizing the need for writing and implementing suitable policies for your setting. Written correctly, policies can help in the smooth running of your business and eliminate misunderstandings. Written badly, and you are set to cause confusion and misinterpretation.

Policies can be written for just about any area of your business but, before putting pen to paper (or fingers to keyboard), it is a good idea to think about what kind of policies you, personally, feel are necessary. It is better to have four or five well-written policies which serve a purpose than to have 20 policies which you have written simply because you know how to write them!

Policies are very personal. They refer to your own setting and will not therefore be the same as those of your colleagues. Your own rules and expectations may well vary, not only from those of other childminders, but also from those experienced by the children at home and it is important that you take this into consideration when writing your policies. This does not mean that if a child is allowed to wear their outdoor shoes indoors at home you have to allow them to do the same in your own home but it does not mean that occasionally, if the child forgets to remove their shoes, they are deliberately disobeying you. Your policies need to be easy to understand as well as simple to implement. They need to be appropriate to the age and level of understanding of the children t and both parents and children need to be aware of their ...istence if you have any hope of implementing them!

Although examples of policies can be found in various forms, in publications and on websites, you would be well advised to use these for information purposes only and to write your own policies from scratch. As I have mentioned before, what is acceptable to one childminder may not be acceptable to another and it is for this reason that each policy should be written individually and from a personal point of view.

Behaviour

Before beginning to write a behaviour policy you will need to ask yourself a few questions and answer them truthfully:

1   What kind of behaviour do you personally feel is unacceptable?

2   How would you like the children in your care to behave?

3   How can you reasonably expect parents to back you in implementing your behaviour policy?

Many of the rules you have with regard to behaviour will depend very much on the age of the children you are caring for and, of course, their level of understanding and you will need to change your policies often to take these factors into account. It is pointless, for example, having a rule which states that all children must say 'please and thank you' if you are caring for children who have not mastered speaking yet! Likewise requesting children to share and take turns will only really be effective for children over the age of two as we all know that children under that age are by nature mean and egotistical!

Behaviour policies therefore must be written carefully and take into account all of the children in your care. Your policy will differ greatly from those of your fellow childminders and, although it may be beneficial to discuss ideas and opinions with your colleagues – often someone else can put a different slant on something and experience may have made them think of things in different terms, which you yourself may not have considered – when it comes to writing your own behaviour policy, this must be tailored to suit your personal requirements.

Confidentiality

Unlike behaviour, a confidentiality policy may well be very similar to those of other childminders as the very nature of this type of policy is to reassure parents that the information they share with you will not be shared with anyone else. Parents may pass on sensitive information to you in confidence and they will need to be certain that the minute they are out of the door you are not going to be on the telephone gossiping about how they have just lost their job or that they suspect their partner is having an affair! If a parent confides in you it is of paramount importance that the information they tell you is kept confidential at all times. Likewise you will need to know how to respond to a parent who asks you questions about another child whom you are caring for or their family. When writing a confidentiality policy you will need to think about:

- The kind of information parents are likely to divulge to you.

- How sensitive this information is.

- How you would deal with a situation if a parent asked you personal information about another child you are caring for or their family.

- How you would deal with a situation if a parent made a

omment or assumption about another child in your care or their family.

Equal opportunity

Discrimination of any kind is a very sensitive subject and one which all childminders must address. It is not acceptable for childminders to ignore or condone inappropriate comments and you will need to know how to respond to issues of discrimination as well as to understand why and how to implement an equal opportunities policy.

All children, regardless of their age, gender, religion, culture, ability, race or skin colour have the right to be treated equally. Many forms of discrimination are at the root of violations of children's rights if they are prevented from active and equal involvement in their community for the reasons I have just listed.

Discrimination is not always obvious and sometimes, as the result of negative assumptions, a person's rights can be ignored. Discrimination can have significant effects on a child's growth and development including:

- Lack of self-esteem
- Lack of confidence
- Feelings of inadequacy
- Struggling to handle pressure
- Struggling to develop friendships
- Feelings of failure
- Reluctance to respond to challenges.

Childminders need to know how to write and implement equal

opportunities policies in order to ensure that *all* the children in their care feel welcomed and valued and they must be confident in ensuring that they are able to challenge any stereotypical situations.

In order to write a successful policy to incorporate equal opportunities you will need to consider the following points:

- What is your own understanding of equal opportunities?

- Would you challenge someone who made a racist comment?

- How would you challenge someone who made a racist comment?

- How do you consider you can reasonably promote equal opportunities successfully whilst childminding?

- Why do you think it is important to promote equality of opportunity whilst childminding?

- What do you hope your policy will achieve?

By answering this last question honestly you should have some idea of what to include in your policy. A policy is not simply something to decorate the walls with. It should contain useful, relevant information which will help with the smooth running of your business.

Sick children

All policies in a childminding setting are important. If they aren't important then they aren't necessary and if they aren't necessary don't waste your time writing them. Rest assured if you think they are irrelevant busy parents with much more on their minds than making your job easier will think exactly the same! Sick child policies are not just relevant, they are essential! You *will* experience problems with regard to caring for sick children if you do not have a policy in place which states clearly and accurately with absolutely no room for misunderstanding exactly what you expect in the case of a sick child. So, if you don't want to end up looking after several children, all ranging in degrees of infection, write your plan and make sure everyone understands it.

If you give in to one parent whose child has a bad dose of flu, rest assured the following week you will be expected to care for children suffering from all kinds of ailments and allergies. You must be firm in your refusal to care for sick children and make sure that parents understand why you have such a policy. Sick child policies are there to protect everyone in the setting. Refusing to care for a sick child is the simplest way of ensuring that the other children in the setting are not exposed to any infection and, of course, that you yourself do not come down with the illness which will prevent you from carrying out your duties altogether.

Parents will not always thank you if you tell them that you don't feel that their child is well enough to be in the setting. They may be annoyed for a number of reasons:

- They may think that their child is not as ill as you do.

- They may think you are questioning their parenting skills.

- They may think you are being difficult or unreasonable.

- It may simply be inconvenient for them to take time off work to care for their child.

Whatever the parents' reaction, it is important that when you have made your decision you stick to it and insist that the child is taken away from the setting. By backing down you not only undermine your own authority you also make the policy you have written pointless and risk the wrath of other parents if their child also succumbs to the illness, which is of course quite likely if you agree to care for a sick child. This is neither ethical nor professional.

When parents disagree with your policies

What happens when a parent refuses to accept one of your policies? How should you respond to a parent who requests that you change your policy to suit them? Are policies set in stone, unable to be changed or amended?

First let us look at the reasons why a parent may refuse to accept one of your policies. It could be that they disagree with a particular area which has little impact on how you see the effects of the policy working, in which case you may well agree to amend it slightly to incorporate the parent's preference; it may be that the policy does not take a particular child's circumstances into account, for example, a disability or cultural issue, in which case you will need to re-evaluate the policy and ensure that everyone's circumstances are considered; or it may simply be that the parent disagrees with you. If this is the case you will need to decide whether the issue is important enough for you to alter your policy. In my opinion if something is important enough to include in a policy and it matters enough to you then you should not back down or allow a parent to 'bully' you into seeing things their way. Once again take into account how many children you are caring for and if, for example, four other parents see no reason to disagree with you, then is it necessary for you to reconsider to please just one? Explaining the reasoning behind a particular rule or policy usually has the desired effect and parents will, albeit sometimes reluctantly, agree if they are encouraged to understand that some rules are necessary and that they are put in place to protect everyone. However if a parent flatly refuses to abide by one of your policies and gives you no justifiable reason for doing so then you must reconsider working with them.

It is always a good idea to write policies for things like behaviour with the children themselves in order for them to let you know what they consider important and for them to explain how they would like to be treated. Always talk over your policies with parents and issue them with a copy of the policies for them to keep and refer back to if necessary. It is also a good idea to get parents to sign to acknowledge that they understand and agree to the policies so you have some kind of 'come back' should issues be raised at a later date. Review your policies periodically to ensure that they remain suitable for the children you are currently caring for and also take into account the needs of any new children entering the setting.

11
Remaining positive

Sometimes it is not easy to remain positive when childminding. You may be stressed, feeling undervalued, tired, busy or simply in need of a change. *All* professions will at times leave you feeling like this and childminders are certainly not alone with their feelings. When the going gets tough are you really going to throw in the towel and look for an easier job, one with less stress and shorter hours? You may well find this kind of job and, for a while, be happy with the change but will it bring about the immense satisfaction that working with children can bring? Will you have the same feelings of pride when you have worked with a parent to solve a particular behaviour issue, helped a child to master certain self-help skills or successfully settled a new child into your setting? Childminding is hard work, demanding and, at times, stressful but no more than any other job where the satisfaction is high and the rewards pleasing.

Although experience brings with it an increase in confidence, less stress and the ability to arrange routines so that they run smoothly, it also brings about a certain amount of complacency – we feel a little too sure in ourselves and our abilities. One of the biggest disadvantages that childminders have is their lack of support from colleagues. Working with another childminder or an assistant helps to keep things in perspective and encourages us to focus on the important issues and to reflect on the way we run our business. All too often childminders working alone tend to fall into a rut and find it hard to motivate themselves and to come up with fresh ideas. When negativity takes hold it is difficult to see the light at the end of the tunnel and minor problems can build up into major catastrophes overnight. This is when a lot of childminders wonder why they bother doing the job they do and, instead of focusing on their love of children and the satisfaction caring for our young generation brings, they end up dissecting something that a parent has said and, after blowing things out of all proportion, they end up throwing in the towel and looking for another job. Usually if we work with colleagues they can help us to snap out of these negative phases in our lives and help us to get things back into perspective. With childminding this is not always a possibility and sometimes we find it difficult to focus on the positive things when the negative are threatening to engulf us.

One of the best ways of remaining positive and tackling each day with renewed vigour and enthusiasm is to ensure that your job remains exciting and challenging. You will need to set yourself targets and goals in order to achieve a certain level of satisfaction and to continue to enjoy the profession you have worked so hard to make a success. Failure to do this will result in your business and your ideas becoming monotonous. If you feel bored at the prospect of childminding every day imagine how the children you are caring for must be feeling!

Feeling fed up and frustrated *some* of the time is par for the course in all professions. However, it is when you have these feelings regularly or all of the time that you need to have a major re-think about your career. Not only are you being unfair to yourself, if you genuinely feel you have come to the end of the line with regard to childminding, you will also be doing the children you care for and their families a great disservice if you carry on childminding knowing full well that your heart isn't in it and you are not performing your duties to your full potential. This is when you should be seriously thinking about a career change. This does not have to be as drastic as it sounds and I have covered career opportunities in more detail in Chapter 12 of this book.

Being a reflective practitioner

Working with children is challenging, demanding and highly rewarding. The job requires a great many skills not least the love and understanding of children and how certain factors influence their lives. Childminders need to be organized and adaptable in order to rise to the many varied challenges they come across on a daily basis. It is absolutely essential that childminders take time out to look at their work and to think about aspects which may need changing or improving in order to build on their experience and knowledge. Childminders need to be *reflective practitioners*.

In order to be a reflective practitioner you will need to look at your business and the service you provide critically. You need to think about the things you do and the methods you use and whether or not any improvements can be made. It is important that you remember that not all criticism is negative and that constructive criticism should be embraced and acted upon. Unless we can look at ourselves and our business practice from a reflective point of view we will fail to move forward, act upon issues or improve the standard of the service we provide.

In order to be a reflective practitioner you will need to:

1   Contemplate what you do. Think carefully about the service you provide and consider which areas you can improve upon.

2   Look at your business logically and be critical of yourself. You will not improve the service you provide if you have an inflated opinion of yourself and feel you cannot improve on the things you are already doing. No one is perfect and even childminding businesses which have been graded as 'outstanding' by Ofsted still need to move forward and build on the good practice they are already providing. If we

stand still and allow things to remain the same then we risk becoming stale.

3 Build on your skills and add to your knowledge at all times. You should never be content with what you know and must continue to look at and access suitable training.

In order to look at your business critically you will need to ask yourself several questions on a regular basis and, more importantly, answer these questions truthfully:

- What areas of my business are my strongest?

- What areas of my business are my weakest?

- Where can I find information to help improve my weakest areas?

- How can I access suitable training?

- How can I alter my routines to improve my business?

- What areas of my business work particularly well?

Being a reflective practitioner is paramount to the success of any business. It will help you to understand what is expected of you, increase your skills and recognize your strengths and weaknesses. It is not always easy to look at ourselves critically and if someone points something out to us that we do not like, we are often unable to accept this as 'constructive criticism', which we can learn from. Nobody likes to be told they are doing things wrong or that their methods are ineffective. However, by taking a step back and looking at things from a totally different viewpoint, we can often see exactly what the other person is getting at and we are then usually well on the way to finding a solution. Admitting that something needs changing is often more difficult than bringing about the changes themselves. Becoming stuck in your ways and refusing to look for fresh ideas will eventually become demoralizing and your job will become boring.

Of course being a reflective practitioner does not simply mean taking on board someone else's criticism and looking at it positively. In order to be reflective we should be questioning ourselves and our ability to carry out our duties on a regular basis. We should never become complacent and think that we have achieved all that is necessary. We can always improve on things and this is why it is important for childminders to evaluate and assess their practice in order for them to move forward and improve on their skills.

It may be that because no one has ever voiced an opinion about your practice you are lulled into a false sense of security. Being of the opinion that everyone is happy with the service you provide and therefore seeing no reason to change anything can be disastrous. Just because you have always done something in a certain way and no one has ever criticized you does not mean that your methods are the best and cannot be improved upon. Sometimes we can become so familiar with a particular routine we take it for granted that because it appears to work well it is the most effective method. However, this is of course not necessarily true. It may be that after evaluating your practice, you bring about changes that are ineffective or which parents and indeed children are not happy with and you may feel that you have made a big mistake. This can rock your confidence and set you back *if* you allow it to. If, on the other hand, you are wise enough to admit when you have made a mistake, and can pick yourself up, dust yourself down and try again then you will have shown true professionalism and understood exactly what it is to be a reflective practitioner! Learning by our mistakes is essential, ignoring them is disastrous! Trying out new methods, even if they prove less effective than the original ones, is much better than not trying them in the first place. Improvements will never be made without a certain degree of risk.

There are of course many areas in which childminders need to be reflective. Every issue, every routine, every policy etc. needs to be carefully looked at periodically and assessed in order to determine whether or not your methods are effective or whether they need changing. Think about your methods for:

- Managing children's behaviour. How do you know whether your methods are working? How can you modify or alter this area of your practice? When does it become apparent that changes need to be made?

- Taking and collecting children from school. Are the children often late for school? Is the morning routine a mad, hectic rush? Do you find it difficult to collect children on time?

- Collecting fees. Do your customers regularly fail to pay you on time? Do you have a problem being paid? Are you unhappy asking for fees?

These are just a few of the many areas of childminding which need to be looked at reflectively in order to determine whether things are working well.

Feeling valued

It is vital that childminders are confident in finding ways of keeping their practice fresh and their ideas fun and exciting. Children need to spend time in a vibrant, lively and exhilarating environment that provides them with educational and fun experiences which they can enjoy and look forward to. Sometimes if a childminder becomes too confident and competent in their work, they can risk 'losing the edge' that initially made their setting so appealing to children and their parents and the days and weeks can then quickly turn boring and predictable. If the childminder finds their work boring and tedious rest assured the children will too and it is important that you do not allow yourself and, more importantly, your ideas to become stale.

In order for you to keep up the enthusiasm you initially had for your business venture it is paramount that you feel valued and that the work you do is appreciated by both the children and their parents. However, if you are waiting for a pat on the back from a busy parent to kick-start your motivation you may be in for a long wait. Although parents are usually quick to comment on how tired and run down you look, rarely will they notice your vigour and ardent enthusiasm for the job you do. Admittedly it is good to have your work appreciated and acknowledged but unfortunately this is a rare occurrence and you will therefore need to ensure that you are able to continue in your chosen profession without the obligatory pat on the back – compliments are an added bonus so don't rely on them!

There will be times when you feel like throwing in the towel in despair and wonder why you bother but it is important that you keep these moments in perspective and remember all the times when you have made progress with a particular child and achieved something that you have been particularly proud of. It is important that you value yourself before looking for others to congratulate you on a job well done. Think about all the times when you have shown a child how to hold a knife and fork correctly and how proud you both were when they successfully mastered the task and managed to eat their lunch without getting most of the food on themselves and the floor. Focus on the positive issues where your work has made a real difference to a child. Remember how you have helped an unhappy child through the months of uncertainty they faced whilst their parents were going through a divorce or the terrible suffering of a child you guided through a phase of bullying at school. All these situations should help you to feel proud that you have achieved a positive outcome and made a real difference to the children's lives. You don't need a certificate or compliments to recognize these kinds of achievements – you just need to remember them and reflect on them when times get tough.

Receiving a complaint

When a parent has cause for complaint it is never an easy time for
the childminder. The nature of the complaint, and how you deal
with it, will have a big effect on the outcome. However it is true to
say that most childminders will be anxious to please their
customers and a complaint can often only be seen negatively.
Always try to keep things in perspective and wherever possible
talk things through with the parents. Apologize if an apology is
necessary and find a suitable solution. Listen carefully to what the
parent is telling you and turn the complaint around so that you
can use it constructively to ensure that you act upon it and
improve the service you provide as a result of it. Criticism should
not always been seen in a negative light and constructive criticism
can be very useful. Always try to see things positively and learn by
your mistakes.

It is true that some people take criticism very personally and this
can make the situation stressful, whereby the childminder may
feel unable to work with the parent in the future. This is a great
shame as, quite often, many minor disagreements can be easily
and satisfactorily resolved if everyone is willing to talk things
through and look for a suitable solution. Avoid 'hanging' on to a
complaint, and when things have been sorted let it go and try not
to dwell on it in the future.

Self appraisal

In order to reflect on the service you provide and to ensure that
your ideas do not become stale or that your motivation does not
wane you may find it beneficial to carry out a self appraisal
periodically. Self appraisal is a way of looking at yourself and your
service constructively and recognizing your strengths and
weaknesses. Your self appraisal could look something like this:

Area for consideration	Strengths	Weaknesses	Action needed
Health history			
Personality			
Reliability			
Organizational skills			
Knowledge			
Experience			
Training			
Commitment			
Assertiveness			

You can add other areas that you feel you personally would benefit from taking into account when carrying out a self appraisal. It is vital that you complete the self appraisal honestly and that you use your findings beneficially. If, after carrying out a self appraisal, you discover that your knowledge in a certain area of childcare, for example, cultural diversity, is poor then you should ensure that you look into how you can access the necessary training. Completing a self appraisal and then filing the outcome is of benefit to no one. Collate your findings, use the information and make the necessary changes!

12

Career opportunities

There is a variety of career options available to individuals with experience in working with young children in an early years setting. Childminders have the added advantage of not only working with young children but also of having the experience of running a small business – something that many childminders take for granted every day. Although caring for children is the primary role of a childminder the business side of things is equally important and it is essential that this is taken care of in a professional manner. Childminders need to be proficient in:

1   Agreeing and writing contracts

2   Planning routines

3   Planning and preparing activities

4   Writing and implementing policies and procedures

5   Keeping up-to-date records for the children

6   Keeping an up-to-date register of the children

7   Accounts and bookkeeping

8   Assessing and monitoring children's progress and development.

Think of all the other jobs you could do with experience in the above fields. Childcare practitioners need to be organized, efficient and remarkably good at multitasking!

Many childminders first enter the business when they become parents themselves. This may be for a number of reasons such as:

- To enable them to stay at home with their own children.

- To enable them to earn an income whilst they are at home with their own children.

- To give their own children friends to play with.

Whatever the reason for deciding on a career change, it is probably true to say that a lot of childminders decide that the time is right to change career paths once their own children have grown up a little and perhaps started school. The reasons for this may be:

1   They no longer wish to work from home.

2   They like the social aspect of returning to the workplace.

3   They no longer wish their home to be full of baby equipment.

4   They feel they have 'outgrown' the role of childminder.

Childminders who feel they have 'outgrown' the role may be doing themselves a great disservice if they decide to take on a different career path simply because they no longer feel fulfilled with childminding or consider the role to be less challenging than it was. These feelings can of course be dealt with, and often by re-evaluating your whole career it is possible to continue with your childminding whilst taking on extra challenges. You may decide to reduce your childminding hours in order to branch out into other things and many childminders alter their business hours to work perhaps three days per week or decide to provide only before and after school childcare and holiday cover in order to give themselves the time to devote to other childcare-related roles such as becoming a:

- Support childminder

- Community childminder

- Accredited childminder

- Tutor

- Network coordinator.

Support childminding

Support childminders are employed by local councils across the country to help newly registered childminders and people going through the registration process. Support childminders offer help, advice and reassurance in the everyday running of the business. Many new childminders are unaware of how to access training courses, and filling in forms and keeping accounts can often be daunting to the inexperienced. Support childminding can be extremely satisfying and enables experienced childminders to meet new people and share their experiences, views and opinions.

Regular meetings with the scheme's coordinators also enable childminders to keep abreast of changes thus helping them to reflect on their own practice. Support childminders need to undergo special training for the role and, as part of the job, they will need to attend meetings as and when required.

Community childminding

Community childminding networks were set up in order to arrange for suitable care for children who have been referred by social services. They may offer temporary full-time care or perhaps respite care for families who are experiencing problems. If you decide to become a community childminder you will need to take extra training that will arm you with the necessary knowledge needed for caring for children in need, or from distressed or vulnerable backgrounds.

Accredited childminding

Accredited childminders, who are members of a Children Come First approved childminding network, are able to offer early years education to three- and four-year-olds. This means that the childminder effectively 'educates' children and supports them in the Foundation Stage of the National Curriculum. In the past many children have left the home-based setting to attend a group nursery provision. However, it is now possible for children to remain in the home-based setting and still receive nursery education from an accredited childminder. Local authorities will pay accredited childminders a 'nursery education grant' for the work they carry out.

Extra training is necessary before a childminder can become accredited and support can be accessed from early years teachers who may be attached to the network.

Tutoring

There are many opportunities for childminders to become tutors. Their experience and approach make them ideal candidates to deliver courses for units in the Diploma in Home-based Childcare. It is always nice to speak to and be trained by a fellow childminder who knows exactly what you are going through and often their experience is invaluable. Many colleges have realized the difficulty childminders have attending classes due to their long working hours and now offer the Diploma in Home-based Childcare as a distance learning course.

Tutoring opportunities may take the form of teaching in class or by distance learning and you will be required to take a qualification in order to enable you to teach adults. Tutoring is a natural progression for many support childminders as they will already have gained invaluable knowledge supporting and advising childminders.

Network coordinator

Many childminders belong to informal childminding networks that are often organized through local childminding groups. These networks are invaluable for offering help and support to one another and many offer a service for holiday and sickness cover. The Children Come First Quality Assurance Network Scheme or local authority-designed networks expand on the principles of these informal networks and, in order for them to run smoothly and be successful, coordinators are required to undertake a variety of roles including:

1   Recruiting registered childminders to the network. In order for a childminder to join a network they need to demonstrate that their current practice meets the National Childminding Association's quality childminding charter standards or, in the case of a local authority network, their own childcare standards.

2   Regularly visiting childminders who are part of the network to monitor their work and ensure that they are maintaining standards.

3   Organizing training for childminders.

4   Providing and arranging suitable training opportunities.

5   Giving help, advice, information and practical support to childminders.

6   Liaising with the Local Education Authority over the provision of education by accredited childminders.

7   Helping parents to find suitable childminders for their family's needs.

8   Helping parents to find alternative care at short notice perhaps due to sickness, holiday or if they have simply been let down.

In addition to the above roles which are centred primarily around childminding you may decide that the time has come for you to leave childminding behind completely and branch out into a totally different area. Your experience in working with children can still go a long way to helping you find alternative employment. If you still like the idea of working with children you might like to consider:

1   Becoming a primary school teacher. Many childminders enrol on courses that will help them to change their careers later on down the line when they decide they have taken their childminding duties as far as they would like. A popular choice is teacher training.

2   Becoming a classroom assistant. Your experience of working with young children will set you in good stead for the role of classroom assistant and, if nothing else, you will understand how demanding young children are prone to be!

3   Becoming a nursery manager. Your wealth of experience of caring for young children, coupled with the management skills gained from running your own business, will set you in good stead to seek employment outside the home, possibly in a nursery. If funds permit you may even like to consider the possibility of opening your own nursery.

4   Early years roles within your local council or working for

Ofsted. Often the skills you have gained through childminding can be used to secure a position with these organizations.

Basically the initial training you have had to become a childminder coupled with the wealth of experience you will have gained whilst working with children and running your own business will set you in good stead for any number of positions, should you wish to take a break from childminding or simply diversify into other fields. With additional training you might like to consider working in:

1 Child protection
2 Child counselling
3 Behaviour management
4 Education.

Index

My Number

07869 677093